REACH BEFORE YOU TEACH

IGNITE PASSION AND PURPOSE
IN YOUR CLASSROOM

Paula Prentis and Chris Parrott

with Amy Smith

CORWIN
A SAGE Company

CORWIN
A SAGE Company

FOR INFORMATION:

Corwin

A SAGE Company

2455 Teller Road

Thousand Oaks, California 91320

(800) 233-9936

www.corwin.com

SAGE Publications Ltd.

1 Oliver's Yard

55 City Road

London EC1Y 1SP

United Kingdom

SAGE Publications India Pvt. Ltd.

B 1/I 1 Mohan Cooperative Industrial Area

Mathura Road, New Delhi 110 044

India

SAGE Publications Asia-Pacific Pte. Ltd.

3 Church Street

#10-04 Samsung Hub

Singapore 049483

Copyright © 2014 by Corwin

Printed in the United States of America

A catalog record of this book is available from the Library of Congress.

ISBN 978-1-4522-6138-6

This book is printed on acid-free paper.

SUSTAINABLE FORESTRY INITIATIVE
Certified Chain of Custody
Promoting Sustainable Forestry
www.sfiprogram.org
SFI-01268
SFI label applies to text stock

Acquisitions Editor: Arnis Burvikovs

Associate Editor: Desirée A. Bartlett

Editorial Assistant: Ariel Price

Production Editor: Amy Schroller

Copy Editor: Lana Arndt

Typesetter: C&M Digitals (P) Ltd.

Proofreader: Victoria Reed-Castro

Indexer: Judy Hunt

Cover Designer: Karine Hovsepian

13 14 15 16 17 10 9 8 7 6 5 4 3 2 1

Contents

Preface

Whatever we decide is the nature of the fully functioning, self-actualizing individual must become at once the goal of education.

—Arthur Combs (1962, p. 2)

A CHILD'S SENSE OF SELF IS OF PARAMOUNT CONCERN

This book details the most important change needed today in our educational system: Developing a strong sense of self in each and every child.

Over the past few decades, an explosion of information illuminating the importance of educating *the whole child* has rallied educators, professionals, and parents to seek change in America's educational system. Standardized testing, extensive memorization, and rigorous schedules don't contribute to the development of lifelong happy, successful, and productive members of society. Educators need tools to effectively reach the whole child.

In addition, middle and high school students need help navigating the ever-changing and challenging climate of identity formation, clouded by personal stress and media overload. Today's students are, on average, overstructured, stressed out, numbing out, overeating, overmedicated, malnourished, and/or sleep deprived and, therefore, are failing to thrive in an educational system burdened by financial crises, high teacher turnover rates, and a lack of direction. Moreover, the shocking teen statistics in this country highlight their inability to effectively cope with their environment. Consider the high suicide rate, profuse alcohol consumption and drug use, high dropout rate, depression and anxiety diagnoses, as well as the obesity and bullying rate increases over the past few decades.

Teens' need for direction, resilience, and confidence has increased during that time, but our capacity to support this need has not kept pace. In fact, through failed education reform efforts, we've crippled students' potentials (Ravitch, 2010). America's overall standing in worldwide education has seen a steady decline (Organization for Economic Cooperation and Development, 2008). Upon graduation, most students do not feel prepared for the workforce, and indeed, employers lament that today's graduates generally lack the innovative critical-thinking skills necessary to lead us into the future (Abeles, 2010).

These teen trends, and their consequences, demand a shift in education geared toward innovative, critical thinking founded on *a solid sense of self*. This book explores the research and provides the necessary tools to achieve this goal. Specifically, this book emphasizes that social emotional learning is an integral component to helping students reach their full potential. It is a pertinent part of developing the 21st century skills (critical thinking and problem solving, communication, collaboration, and creativity and innovation), character development, and other relevant proactive strategies whose common denominator includes a solid sense of self.

By "self" we mean each child's sense of both separate identity (who I am internally) and his or her relationship to others (who I am externally), as well as aptitudes, interests, concerns, beliefs, fears, and all the characteristics that make a person unique. The information and lessons you teach are less potent when students lack a framework and an image of the self. Indeed, this is why teens often make poor decisions even though information has been provided (posting questionable pictures on Facebook after the character education program, sniffing glue after an antidrug program, sitting in silence when a peer is being tormented after the antibullying talk). The information from these prevention programs is still "floating"—it is not readily accessible because without a self-concept, it has yet to find resonance in the self.

Developing and understanding the self—the emotional, social, physical, *and cognitive* elements of the self—are the critical components teachers need to address in order to reach and support the whole child. Extensive research, as well as interviews with teachers and with students, leaves no doubt that when the self is busy trying to manage social, emotional, and physical challenges, academics suffer (Immordino-Yang & Damasio, 2007).

How are you nurturing the self (each child's individual identity) into lesson plans? How is that nurturing received? You may supply information in the form of brilliant lessons and powerful prevention programs, but without offering students a means to identify with and incorporate their own sense of self, those lectures won't be nearly as effective as you wish them to be. When you incorporate the self into your teaching, you convey the message: *You matter. I care about you and how I can help you become the best person you can be.* With this message, your teaching and students' grades will flourish because the social and emotional needs of the developing student are supported. *After all, students' sense of self provides the strength and confidence to manage external and internal influences so they can focus on what you are teaching.* This book will cite many examples of this important fact.

Furthermore, the teen years provide an ideal opportunity to cement the formation of the self. Identity development is a natural process that begins at birth but is also the hallmark of the teen years. This enormously important process, replete with potential hazards, is rarely addressed in school, which is why most students are unable to concentrate on academics: They lack the self skills to manage their social, emotional, and physical challenges, changes, and selves. We rarely check in with students and address their identity development needs. We rarely provide tools to facilitate and help them shape the process. *That is why we have written this book: It is your toolbox to help your students more confidently tackle identity (self) development so they may feel worthy and fulfilled while finding success academically and personally.*

You may be thinking that this is a job for your mental health team, and indeed, much of it may be. Unfortunately, mental health expenditure has largely been reduced, resulting in fewer resources and personnel. With this present administrative reality, you face your reality: Your students need your help not just in academics, but also in navigating their mental health and identity development. The tools and strategies found in this book help manage the "self" sitting behind the desk, playing on the sports field, and vying for a place to sit in the cafeteria. Weaving self skills into your style of connecting with and relating to your students provides them with a stronger self-concept and a better ability to manage life's ups and downs. Through classroom scenarios and anecdotal evidence, *this book shows you how to develop those skills,* demonstrating that when you bring the self into the classroom, everyone benefits.

THE FOCUS AND PURPOSE OF THIS BOOK

The purpose of this book is twofold. The first purpose is to introduce the idea that social emotional learning curriculums are necessary to help our future generations find their individual successes and passions in life, but *the key to those programs' success is in developing a sense of self.* When the self is supported and developed, students are more apt to reach their full potential because they have been provided a meaning in context: the bread for the butter—the *who-I-am* in the lecture, program, or class. Just by reaching and nurturing the self, you will ignite passion, purpose, and academic progress in your students (Blodget, 2009; Combs, 1962; Eisner, 2004).

The second purpose of this book is to inspire you to start incorporating the self into your curriculum and school climate using the steps and suggested interventions found throughout this book. To this end, each chapter provides teacher examples of interventions at work and concludes with a chart to help you map out how you will apply this information into your classroom.

A Peek at the Steps to Success

Step 1: Understand and connect with the self behind the desk.

Step 2: Soften defenses to foster academic and personal growth.

Step 3: Provide tools for emotional management.

Step 4: Use cognitive understanding to awaken potentials.

Step 5: Consolidate the self in the social world.

Step 6: Support the physical self for optimal overall health.

Step 7: Create an environment that works for you.

Chapters 1 and 2 introduce the idea that a sense of self is a critical factor toward feeling success and happiness both in and out of school. These chapters review the fundamentals of social emotional learning (SEL), including what it is and why it's important; how teaching to the self goes beyond SEL limits; and how the self is influenced by early attachments and making connections.

Chapters 3 through 7 break down the four components of the self (emotional, social, cognitive, and physical) and provide anecdotal illustrations of what is happening within each aspect during the teen years. These chapters also provide examples, illustrations, and charts to help you incorporate the interventions and strategies provided.

Chapter 8 discusses the opportunities within your school climate to effect change. What do your students see as they walk down the hall? How are they affected by attitudes, artwork, and interactions? How is school morale? Simple and affordable ideas for your school climate are offered.

Chapter 9 summarizes previous chapters' purposes and explains how a sense of self aids in motivation, decision making, and a future ripe with potential for giving back to society at large.

In every chapter, we will discuss the topic at hand using research, quotes, explanations, analogies, and levity when needed. Classroom scenarios, input from teachers, and even some feedback from students themselves illustrate the core strategies and points. What is working? What is not? We believe you will begin to see that what "works" is always founded on supporting and validating the self.

Many of the skill sets and interventions suggested may appear to impinge upon your already busy schedule and the necessary standards and mandates you strive to meet. However, please keep in mind that we are familiar with the Common Core State Standards, 21st Century Skills, National Health Standards, and the state mandates aimed at prevention. Teaching to the self, in and of itself, aligns with many of these standards and mandates while reducing the amount of time you ultimately spend on matters that impede your progress in the classroom. Indeed, it buys you time, expanding the potential of your teaching.

The Benefits and Features of This Book

- Details seven straightforward, easy to implement steps to ignite passion and purpose in your classroom
- Demonstrates the ethical necessity to reach the whole child and foster his or her potentials socially, emotionally, physically, and cognitively
- Includes a plethora of real-life teacher illustrations showing the power and impact of the tools and strategies given
- Provides over 50 interventions to reach and connect with each student in your classroom, particularly those students who seem to defy your previous attempts at connection and instruction
- Offers techniques and strategies to form authentic connections with students and explains why these connections you create can mean the difference between thriving students and those who drop out
- Incorporates opportunities to check in with yourself to develop awareness as to how your habits and views impact your teaching style
- Details the functions and structure of the brain and offers ideas on how to share this information with your students
- Explains how social emotional skills and focusing on the self will foster 21st century skills

THIS BOOK APPLIES TO EDUCATORS OF TEENS

This book is primarily geared toward people who work with middle and high school students, specifically

- Teachers
- Teachers in training

- All school mental health professionals (counselors, nurses, psychologist, social workers)
- Administration
- Principals

The philosophy and tone of the book is broad reaching: Though written for educators of teens, much of the content will also benefit teachers of younger children.

Like many educators (and family members and students), you may be feeling a sense of frustration with the direction our education focus has taken in recent history. But hopefully, that frustration is dwarfed by your determination to make change possible. Change *is* possible, and this book is the first step toward helping you create that much-needed change: Change in the way students are approached, taught, addressed, and treated in an effort to bring forth the self, reduce problematic behavior, and improve overall performance.

When you develop a sense of self among your students, you provide the framework and foundation for what they ultimately need to find purpose, success, and happiness in their lives.

Indeed, with tragedies such as the one that occurred at Sandy Hook Elementary School, our culture is beginning to recognize that the mental health of our students must be integrated into our curriculums just as reading, writing, and arithmetic are. Mental health is integral to learning. It profoundly affects learning potential and, indeed, can change the course of a life. Many teachers are already shifting toward a new consciousness in pedagogy—teaching with the self in mind. They have seen for themselves when the whole child is integrated, involved, and present in the classroom, not only do academics improve, but life just feels all that much more hopeful and promising. We share many teacher stories within this book so that, as you see the new ground before you, you will know it is a safe place to land.

THE BOTTOM LINE

In 1962, in the book *Perceiving, Behaving, Becoming: A New Focus for Education*, Arthur Combs stated, "There is often a wide gap between our understanding of the nature of human behavior on the one hand and the utilization of such understanding in the classroom on the other" (p. 2).

Let's not allow another 50 years to pass before we realize and utilize the impressive findings in the fields of neuroscience, psychology, the self, and SEL as they relate to education. Instead, let's focus on the link between these fundamental assets so that you—the educator, mental health professional, or principal—may find a strategic balance that cultivates success within your institution.

We recommend reading this book if you want to

- learn about the self and how it is the key component to successful lifelong learning
- learn proactive strategies to curb potential mental health issues
- learn easy, practical ways to bring the self into your classroom; and
- improve the cognitive, social, emotional, and physical outcomes for your students so they become purposeful, successful learners, and contributing members of society.

Acknowledgments

Acknowledgments From Paula Prentis and Chris Parrott

We wish to thank all the students at Fox Lane Middle School in Bedford, NY, who have been the driving force behind the work that we do and who have helped us develop insight into the minds and hearts of teens. Erin Filner and Amanda Gerber have given time, commentary, and reflection simply because they, too, want the best for our future generations. Mary Beth Staropoli and Deb Dormady have also shared that vision and supported our work tirelessly. Thank you!

Thank you, Amy Smith, for your endless help on content, grammar, and simply the right thing to do or say throughout the book. Your educational experience is priceless. We wish to thank the staff at Corwin, especially Desirée Bartlett, who found Paula at a convention and sparked this wonderful journey, and Arnis Burvikovs for her continued support and wisdom along the ride.

Both of our families have been tremendous in this undertaking. They lost many hours of our time, and we thank them for handling the demands of our schedules so gracefully. Our families encourage and inspire us to be the best that we can be. Thank you for being who you are—humorous, loving, and the joy of our lives.

Acknowledgments From Amy Smith

"Follow your bliss" was Joseph Campbell's recommendation for a motivated, energetic, and successful career. I would like to thank Ramapo High School for the ability to do that and for the compelling experiences I had in the classroom as well as in the Media Center. Working with young adults for so many years was engaging and rewarding, and I feel privileged to have had such a fulfilling career.

I thank the Ramapo faculty for demonstrating wonderful and productive ways to facilitate growth in their students, both in knowledge and in character. I witnessed myriad examples of what is wonderful about the teaching experience when teachers understand and nourish the whole student.

I would also like to thank Dr. Thomas Gorman for his friendship and his vision and the many conversations we had about education. Ridgewood High School is fortunate to have him in a leadership position where he can promote his exceptional insights into young adult education.

Finally, I thank Paula and Chris for the opportunity to participate in the production of a salient and essential book for educators. I know that it will have a positive and discernible impact on the teaching experience.

PUBLISHER'S ACKNOWLEDGMENTS

Corwin wishes to acknowledge the following peer reviewers for their editorial insight and guidance.

Judy Chan, Elementary School
  Teacher
P.S. 124 M
New York, NY

Ann Marie Dargon, Assistant
  Superintendent of Schools
Westport Community Schools
Westport, MA

Nancy Foote, Teacher
Higley Unified School District
San Tan Elementary
Gilbert, AZ

Karen Landress, Speech/Language
  Pathologist
MILA Elementary School
Merritt Island, FL

Helane Smith Miller, Guidance and
  Counseling Department
Ballou STAY
Washington, DC

Susan "Ernie" Rambo, History and
  Future City Educator
Walter Johnson Jr. High School
Las Vegas, NV

Steve Reifman, National Board
  Certified Teacher, Author, and
  Speaker
Roosevelt Elementary School
Santa Monica, CA

Cherie Rose Reissman, Literacy
  Coach and Corwin Author
New York City Department of
  Education
New York, NY

Diane P. Smith, School Counselor,
  Grades 7–12
Smethport Area School District
Smethport, PA

William Sommers, Principal
Spring Lake Park High School
Spring Lake Park, MN

Brigitte Tennis, Headmistress
Stella Schola Middle School
Redmond, WA

Janice Wyatt-Ross, Assistant
  Principal
Cardinal Valley Elementary
Lexington, KY

About the Authors

Paula Prentis was a conflict resolution counselor and a rape crisis counselor in New York City before earning her master's degree in social work (MSW) at New York University. Later, she continued training at Westchester Institute for Psychoanalysis and Psychotherapy and worked in private practice. Prentis is certified in past life regression therapy and continues her professional interests through workshops, lectures, and conferences in neuroscience and the mind/body connection.

In addition, with Chris Parrott, Prentis is the coauthor of the *Your Self Series* of books and website. *Your Self Series* is a curriculum that facilitates teen identity development and is taught as part of an advisory class, a health class, or an after-school program.

Prentis and Parrott lecture nationwide on issues pertaining to teens and mental health in schools. They continually update and populate the *Your Self Series* website with relevant teen information and lesson plans for educators. They have three other products that all aim to influence children to be the best they can be while combating obesity and improving overall health and well-being: YourChatMat.com; YourStacs; and HealthyStacs.

Chris Parrott earned her bachelor's degree with a psychology major at Dartmouth and went on to study counseling psychology at the City University in London, England, where she earned both her master's and postmaster's degrees, and the distinguished title of the British Psychological Society (BPS) Chartered Counseling Psychologist. She also has a diploma in hypnosis from London University. Parrott has published various articles in *Counseling Review Quarterly* and chapters in psychology training books, and she has coauthored a book titled *Doing Therapy Briefly.* Parrott was also a media consultant on behalf of the BPS and has been quoted in *The Times, The Look,* and *The Daily Express.*

 **Amy Smith** was a high school English teacher for over 15 years in the states of Texas, California, and New Jersey, which gave her a diverse experience within the educational sector and a broad spectrum of teacher contacts. Working as an English teacher and, later, as a media specialist for another 15 years, Smith's primary focus was always on the individual spirit of each student who passed through her doors—or walked onto her court: She acted as tennis coach for several years alongside her teaching. Indeed, her passion for her students led her to numerous conventions and professional development seminars over the years where she expanded both her knowledge and contacts. Now retired, Smith enjoys time with her partner, two daughters, and grandson while continuing to look for opportunities to positively affect teen education.

The Self

Know thyself.

—Socrates, Third Century BC

WHAT YOU WILL LEARN IN THIS CHAPTER

In this chapter, you will learn

- What we mean by the "self"
- What the self looks like in school
- How teaching to the self correlates with social emotional learning (SEL)
- How a sense of self contributes to personal success and to society
- What the seven steps to success are

WHAT DO WE MEAN BY THE "SELF"?

When we talk about "teaching to the self," we are talking about connecting with the unique being of each one of your students. To do that, however, one must first understand what the self is. To understand the concept of the self, imagine someone gives you a gray-colored box filled with puzzle pieces. You open the box, and your go-to solution of separating flat edges from the jagged becomes defeating, for no flat edges exist in the box. Stranded with no picture of what the puzzle is supposed to look like and no flat edges to construct a frame, you may feel lost as to how to move forward. Yet, this is precisely what we ask of our teens. We ask them to build an identity without fully discussing with them what identity is or what it is supposed to look like. We don't let them see the picture on the box. We ask them to apply information to a seemingly vacuous concept. We also often fail to help them to build the framework of the puzzle, the fundamentals of themselves. We rarely delve deep into discussions of their values, morals, goals, dreams, feelings, and thought processes—all of which help them be better students and lead more fulfilling and purposeful lives.

As you give students puzzle pieces such as math, science, prevention programs, English, and health, you are asking them to find a place inside of themselves where that piece will fit. But our current system has failed to provide students with a framework for the self. Students cannot incorporate those pieces without a framework.

Defining the Self

self n.

1. The total, essential, or particular being of a person; the individual.
2. The essential qualities distinguishing one person from another; individuality. ("Self," 2011)

The self is your essential being. It is comprised of all your likes, dislikes, wants, desires, needs, opinions, and beliefs. It is the core of your being. It is what makes you *you*—distinct, separate, and unique from all other beings on this planet.

Your experiences (past and present), as well as how you respond to them, shape who you are. The self perceives events, interprets experiences, and changes with each accordingly. You are in a constant state of change. Indeed, your very cell structure and synaptic connections have shifted since you began this chapter. Your self combines all the aspects of who you are and weaves them into the fabric of your every decision, echoing and reinforcing your self to the world. Hence, knowing who you are—being in touch with the consciousness of your self—empowers you to take control of not only how you perceive the past, but also how you handle the present and prepare for the future. Developing this concept in students is invaluable.

The Self as a Container

Imagine that you are born with a container at the center of your solar plexus that represents who you are. This is your core sense of self. Your container is unique to you. As you grow, elements such as upbringing, culture, morals, genetic underpinnings, experiences, and all the things that make you *you*, go into the container and affect its condition, creating a unique self-representation (the container).

The relationship between container and contents is cyclical: What we put into the container permeates the walls of the container either strengthening or corroding its structure/condition. When contents of positive self beliefs permeate the container, they build a stronger overall self-concept (container) that we carry with us. However, the opposite is also true: Contents of negative perceptions about our selves can leach into the container walls and weaken its condition, leaving us with a core self-perception that is tarnished and corroded.

Hence, one person may imagine her container as a shiny platinum vessel with a firm and resilient bottom and sides impervious to outer elements. This is the result of contents that are self-affirming and provide a positive outlook on life, love, and work. With this belief, the self would be open to positive comments while prone to analyze, but not take personally, critical comments. However, another person may envision his container as a rusty old coffee can, choked with barnacles, where beatings and mistreatment have eroded potentials and rust has created a toxic internal environment (see the following illustration). These contents are negative self-perceptions that reap an often dissatisfying existence. Most people's containers resemble something between the two.

The container to the left looks worn, damaged, and leaking. The container on the right looks strong, polished, and resilient. What do the containers in your classroom look like?

Your students' containers are being filled and formed with each and every moment spent in your classroom. As a result, your interactions with them are primed to either continually polish or tarnish their containers. Will they hold onto your positive statements or reject them like a sieve, dismissing any potential for growth? What contents will you contribute to help build the container? Are you securing the base with words of enthusiasm and support? Do you help polish the container, removing barnacles of doubt? Do you fill it with positive experiences and hope? From this day forward, what will you choose to contribute?

Each student, regardless of age, has a container within him or her that represents his or her self-perceptions from years of external and internal influences. These self-representations embody all components of the self. This is why educating the whole self is so important—we can't leave any part of the container vulnerable to corrosion.

Four Components of the Self

What does the self look like? What are its essential elements? As the following diagram illustrates, the core of one's being is where the social self, the emotional self, the cognitive self, and the physical self intersect (other aspects of the self exist—spiritual, moral, cultural, etc.—but are not discussed in detail here). At the central point of intersection, strength is paramount. A weak structure here compromises the integrity of the other components of the self. Just as our bodies rely on core spine strength and stability for the health and flexibility of our limbs, the health of our self relies on a strong intersection of all these self elements.

Indeed, a strong, balanced, and integrated core opens the pathways toward awareness, curiosity, passion, and purpose. What does the core of your student population look like? How will you help your students to find their inner selves and strengthen their cores? With a strong inner core/container

- Social issues don't cloud academic and life progress
- Emotional pain feels manageable
- The physical self supports life desires
- Cognition opens and creativity is enhanced
- Decisions resonate with who we are

Our physical, social, emotional, and cognitive selves overlap to form our core sense of self. When we are aware of each aspect, our core becomes strong and stable, giving us strength.

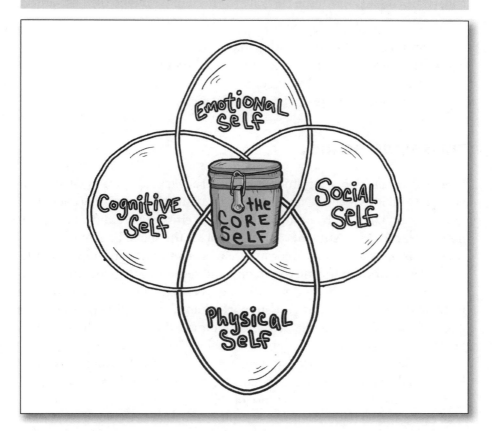

The following chapters explore each aspect of the self by providing understanding, illustration, contemplation, and strategies for intervention. Each chapter summary facilitates your transition from reading to application by including self-reflections on the topics as well as providing charts to facilitate integration and application of the information.

Repair of the Self

This book helps you not only identify the various states in which you find your students' sense of self, but provides various strategies for repair and intervention. Repair of the self often comes from others expressing empathy and compassion, although many other reparative interventions are offered in this book. Throughout these pages, you will be given insights into how the self forms, what can go astray, and what to do about it. In the end, you will be able to elevate the spirit of learning in your classroom and throughout your school simply because you have learned how to allow the self in your students to grow and be present.

When we teach to the self, we empower students not just with cognitive capabilities but also with the capacity to check in with who they are and

- Say no to dangerous influences
- Stand up to abusive relationships
- Make decisions that reflect positive self-concepts
- Foster strong social connections
- Find their passions and interests in life

THE SELF IN SCHOOL

Would you describe your students as distracted and unmotivated or as engaged and attentive? What motivates students to go to school each day? Is it to study Latin verb conjugations or to recite the periodic table of elements? Hardly. Most students enjoy school for the social benefits it affords them. It is a place of self-exploration via peer interaction. Indeed, identities develop through the mirror images and responses the students experience both with their peers and with you. As such, you play a pivotal role in their development: You can support them in their identity search or allow them to fumble along. With no guidance, their positive interactions are left to the whims of the numerous other self-searching students.

Typically, students have two *primary* sources of distraction in school. First, social distractions such as peer pressure weigh on them, albeit to different degrees. Without a solid sense of self, that pressure can become overwhelming and lead to risk taking and other maladaptive coping responses. Second, emotional distractions, such as divorce, trauma, or family demands, hinder performance by rendering students frozen in time, ruminating over their difficulties. A strong sense of self is critical to coping, overcoming and, indeed, growing from these common distractions.

To take a closer look at how the social self can impede academic and life success, imagine bringing an antidrug program to your school. It appears successful in school; students are engaged and receptive. That weekend at a party, however, Jeff may cognitively *think, Wait! I learned that this stuff is bad for me.* But now, living the peer pressure, he *feels* inadequate to follow through with the lessons learned in the program. Why? Because his self was not activated during the antidrug program, and therefore, he did not integrate the material as part of his identity. The self is the governing body that chooses what will have meaning and therefore will influence all subsequent decisions (it *makes* the decisions). One needs a strong self-concept to say inwardly, *I am not a person who takes drugs and I have the strength to stand up to peer pressure.*

People with fully aware, open, and positive self-concepts observe the actions of others and choose how others will influence them. They are able to make decisions by checking in with their selves, not by checking in with the crowd. People with poor self-concepts take things personally, self-sacrifice, join the crowd, and stunt their potential to make good social decisions.

The emotionally distracted student is likewise less likely to reach his academic and life potential. When teaching or giving important information to your students, the hope is that Johnny, or Suzie, or Nadia, or Abdul is actually listening, comprehending, and absorbing. This, however, *assumes* that Johnny (or Suzie . . .) has a solid self structure; that Johnny's not worried about his mother's alcohol problem; that Nadia is not ruminating over the last text message she read; or that Abdul isn't planning his next defense from a bully. Some students orbit the planet (while others inhabit it), not because they don't understand you, but because they lack the capacity to manage the other 18 things happening in their lives that distract them. Without emotional awareness and an ability to manage emotions, your students' chances for learning decrease while their stress levels and chances of dropping out increase—dramatically (Blair, 2012). A decrease in social and emotional distraction goes hand in hand with an increase in student engagement and academic success. Providing both an understanding of the causes of distraction and the tools to foster engagement and motivation is what this book hopes to achieve.

But, what do we mean by teaching to the self? How is it different from our teaching of today? How does it look in the classroom? For us, the question is not so much how it *looks* in the classroom, but how it sounds and feels to each student. Teaching to the self is expressed in the words spoken, the tone of voice used, the approaches taken in problem solving, and the overriding outlook that will drive your decisions in all aspects of your teaching.

Teaching to the self is a philosophy that, when utilized, will pervade your classroom and your perspective far more effectively than a few tricks that will "get students in line." When you teach, you are reaching a social, emotional, cognitive, and physical human who is grappling with myriad changes and influences aimed toward identity development. You are teaching in a classroom filled with containers representing a mosaic of self-perceptions. They are colorful, wild, tame, muted—you name it. How you approach your teaching and the classroom atmosphere you create will influence those budding personalities.

With each intervention listed, the ultimate goal is to reach your students' core self. Programs that develop self-reflection and social and emotional skills (to be addressed shortly) have proved to be highly effective in helping students manage their behaviors and attend to academics. When students have your full attention, they learn more. This seems intuitive, but such a state is not always easy to attain.

We need to reach before we can teach.

To reach students takes a shift in our current perceptions—from simply transferring information from our brain to their notes (did the information linger long enough in their prefrontal cortex to enter their consciousness?) to connecting with our students so that meaning, passion, and purpose are created. It is in these connections that transformation takes place.

Teacher Illustration 1.1: The Importance of Reaching Students

Lorraine Skeen is a retired principal of Patrick Henry School, P.S. 171 in Manhattan, NY, which ranked as one of the lowest-performing schools when she began. Twenty years later, under her vision, P.S. 171 had the lowest rate of failure of several hundred zoned inner-city schools.

The relationship between teachers and students impacts student learning. Students need clear expectations along with strong emotional supports. These are intertwined. Under an older paradigm, this would be subsumed under the broad and often ill-defined umbrella of classroom management. At its best, this would include positive ways to motivate, engage, and support ego strength in order for a student to view himself or herself as a successful learner. At a young age, the development of a healthy self-concept through positive reinforcement is stressed. I have seen this meaningful support enhance student capacity for learning. Too often this is not a part of the approach used with older students.

SOCIAL EMOTIONAL LEARNING: ITS IMPORTANCE AND HOW THE SELF ENABLES SEL POTENTIAL

We believe that strengthening a student's feeling of well-being, self-esteem, and dignity is not an extra curriculum. If anything, a student's sense of belonging, security, and self-confidence in the classroom provides the scaffolding that supports the foundation for enhanced learning, engagement, motivation, self-discipline, responsibility, and the ability to deal more effectively with obstacles and mistakes.

—Robert Brooks (2012)

Social emotional learning (SEL), in our opinion, is one of the greatest shifts in pedagogical consciousness in decades. Maurice Elias and Joseph Zins (2006), leading authors and contributors to the field of SEL, describe SEL as the "capacity to recognize and manage emotions, solve problems effectively, and establish positive relationships with others, competencies that clearly are essential for all students" (p. 1).

Social emotional programs work. Dr. Joseph A. Durlak and his team conducted a meta-analysis of 213 school-based, universal SEL programs and discovered the importance of addressing the social and emotional needs of today's youth: "Compared to controls, SEL participants demonstrated significantly improved social and emotional skills, attitudes, behavior, and academic performance that reflected an 11-percentile-point gain in achievement" (Durlak, Weissberg, Dymnicki, Taylor, & Schellinger, 2011). Additionally, when SEL programs were implemented properly, Durlak et al. (2011) found an increase in graduation rates and a decrease in bullying behavior.

Researchers are not the only ones convinced. Teachers have also strongly weighed in on the issue. At the 2013 Collaborative for Academic, Social and Emotional Learning (CASEL) Forum, the results of A National Teacher Survey on How Social and Emotional Learning Can Empower Children and Transform Schools were shared. Key findings include the following:

- Nearly all teachers (93%) believe SEL is very or fairly important for the in-school student experience.
- Nearly all teachers (95%) believe social and emotional skills are teachable and report that SEL will benefit students from all backgrounds, rich or poor (97%).
- More than three-quarters of the teachers believe a larger focus on SEL will be a major benefit to students because of the positive effect on workforce readiness (87%), school attendance and graduation (80%), life success (87%), college preparation (78%), and academic success (75%).
- 8 in 10 teachers think that SEL will have a major benefit on students' ability to stay on track and graduate and that it will increase standardized test scores and overall academic performance (77%).
- Of the teachers who view negative school climate as a problem, 80% view SEL as a solution. ("The Missing Piece," n.d.)

A shift in education is needed: a shift toward focusing on the development of the child's sense of self. Indeed, today's educational approach must foster social and emotional growth and weave well-designed programs aimed at building *the self* into curriculum. When we teach these skills, we enable students to understand, manage, and express the social and emotional aspects of their lives in ways that help them to make smart decisions, whether in personal relationships, life, or work.

SEL and the notion of teaching to the self agree in the importance of creating socially, morally, and civically minded people who contribute to society; people capable of social awareness and emotional management; people who are healthy, cognitively and physically. How then do you teach so that these markers are attainable? Such teaching requires more than developing a set of skills; it requires knowing how those skills work together and the impact such skills will have on identity. This larger framework is precisely the goal of teaching to the self and one that further complements the SEL approach.

The self chooses and defines who we are and, in order to make sound decisions, often checks in with the social and emotional skills mentioned here. *However, the complete self understands not only its social and emotional self, but its deeply centered self—the who-am-I?—in each and every scenario presented.* The self knows who it is in relation to nearly any conceivable situation because the essence of the self is consciously available. For example, reflecting on "Who am I in relation to drugs and alcohol?" has a stronger impact on the outcome of a drug prevention program because the self was part of the learning process and incorporated the material as part of the identity. Furthermore, knowing about yourself aids in decision making (see Chapter 9). When making a decision, all the nuances and contributing factors pertaining to the self are pondered, reflected upon, and incorporated into the subsequent decisions—decisions that reflect the self.

SEL skills and teaching to the self work in tandem, but with slight differences: Take a moment to imagine that you are from a different planet. When you arrive here on earth, you are taught many different skills for your survival. You are taught how to wire for electricity, install sheet rock, create plumbing, lay foundation, etc.—all extremely useful skills, but all just singular disconnected skills until someone connects their central purpose: that with all these skills you can build a home. What type of home, how large, the layout, everything about it, is in your control. But, being from another planet, you would not know that you could build a home until someone pulled all those skills together for you and showed you their interlocking purpose.

The self provides a larger framework for incorporating all sorts of skills, programs, and core subjects. Whether it be leadership, mathematics, ethics, antibullying, drug prevention, or reading, until we teach students how these skills relate to the self, we fail to help them see, let alone build, their new homes—their self. As a result, they are left building a structure that is often put together haphazardly, without a well-thought-out framework, blueprint, or design.

We wish for every teen to have a strong sense of self: a well-designed "home" that expresses his or her unique style while also giving that teen shelter and protection from the outside world. In teaching to the self, we are attempting to reach each student at "home" where he or she is apt to feel safest, and to help each student build a structure that will serve him or her well and, ultimately, one that will welcome others.

Whether you are teaching academics, leadership programs, character development, antibullying, or nutrition, the greater your students' sense of self, the more likely they will retain information and find it meaningful and relevant. SEL programs are an integral part of this journey, but an integrated self-concept, one that will help them to continually remodel and furnish their "home" in a way that resonates with who they are is essential.

HOW DOES A SENSE OF SELF CONTRIBUTE TO PERSONAL SUCCESS AND TO SOCIETY?

The U.S. Department of Education (2011) reported the 2009 dropout rate at 8.1%. This means that every day nearly 7,000 students become dropouts. Each year, 1.2 million students will not graduate high school. Though many students drop out in order to financially help their families, a large proportion of students drop out for other reasons. According to a National Longitudinal Study conducted by the U.S. Department of Education Statistics, a summary of reasons why eighth- and tenth-grade students dropped out broken down into categories includes the following:

School related

51% did not like school

35% could not get along with teachers

39.9% were failing school

Job related

14.1% needed to work

15.3% had to get a job

15.3% found a job

Family related

51% were pregnant

13.6% became pregnant

13.1% got married (Bridgeland, DiIulio, & Morison, 2006)

These reasons are related to the self. Sometimes teachers are unable to make a connection with the self behind the desk (Chapter 2). Sometimes students make decisions that result in them dropping out, the consequences of which have a ripple effect on society, family, and the nation. More than 12 million students will drop out in the next 10 years, resulting in a loss to the nation of $3 trillion (U.S. Department of Education, 2011). But, it's not our nation that suffers the most; it is the human toll of lost potential, a terrible waste of possibility as well as productivity. (For more information on costs to society, see Chapter 9.)

Students who drop out do so usually because they don't feel a connection to a person at school or to the material at hand. Left without feeling connected and dropping out, they head off into the world to develop relationships, find work, and perhaps eventually raise children. Feeling no connections, what will be the quality of their lives? The quality of their work? What will be the quality of the parenting they give? What are the chances of connectedness and life satisfaction for that next generation they raise? Academic success alone does not guarantee life success and happiness. In fact, feeling connected and engaged are greater indicators of life happiness than financial success (Seligman, 2011). By teaching to the self, you support and develop connection, confidence, and academics equally.

> **Check In With Your Self**
>
> Will developing a positive relationship with your students enhance or distract from your teaching? Their learning? Do you have an example of each?

Twenty-First Century Changes

School is not about merely transferring information from one brain to the next. If it were, we'd be robots—void of emotion, stimulation, grit, and spark. Today, we have technology and other sources to help us obtain infinite amounts of information. But how do we learn what to do with all this information? How do we transform it into innovative ideas that aid humankind? What information are we teaching to propel students toward their goals while meeting the demands of the globally competitive world? Today, teachers are being asked to teach the skills necessary to manipulate the information and apply it to a larger framework for common good. We call this 21st century skill development.

That development is enhanced, indeed becomes exponential, with the discovery of personal meaning: *How does this information fit with who I am or the goals I have for myself?* Teaching to the self increases the possibility that personal meaning will be discovered: Teaching to the self allows the self to feel safe and open to exploring new material and incorporating it into one's self-perceptions.

We believe (and Socrates would agree) that asking questions is at the heart of eliciting insight and motivation. Open-ended questions involve the self and therefore spur reflection and forward movement. With this concept in mind, we wanted to share with you a section from Folwell Dunbar (2008), school leader at Young Audiences Charter School, New Orleans, LA, from his article "Essential Questions: Mining for Understanding":

A Question-Marked Curriculum

So, how do we venture beyond trivial pursuits? With apologies to self-help books and the Dalai Lama, the answer *is* the question. Most questions posed to students in schools are of the forced choice variety—the child is *forced* to *choose* a predetermined **correct** answer. What is the capital of El Salvador? Who wrote the Declaration of Independence? If a train left the station . . . what time would it arrive? While they are not always *trivial*, they do often elicit the response, "Who cares?" or "Does it really matter?" Not to mention, "I could have easily found this on Wikipedia." (Insert your own expletive or punctuation mark for emphasis.) As Emeril Lagasse would say, we need to "kick it up a notch!" and convert a percentage of our forced choice questions into essential ones: What can be done to bring political stability to countries like El Salvador in the developing world? What truths today are *truly* and universally self-evident? Planes, trains, or automobiles? What are the pros and cons for different modes of transportation?

Essential questions, also known as umbrella or driving questions, go far deeper than the classroom norm. According to Dr. Jamie McKenzie, they "reside at the top of Bloom's Taxonomy. They spark our curiosity and sense of wonder. They derive from some deep wish to understand something which matters to us. Students must construct their own answers and make their own meaning from the information they have gathered. They create insight." Grant Wiggins adds, "They provide focus for a lesson or unit of study and help reveal a subject's richness and complexity."

Indeed, Dunbar's focus on essential questions supplies a shift in consciousness: from "repeat the right answer" to "what do *you* think?" They engage the cognitive mind and also support the self. When we do this, the probability increases that the mental health of students will thrive along with their cognitive abilities.

STEPS TO SUCCESS—FOR TEACHING AND FOR YOU

Successful Teaching to the Self

Why read this book if you can't slip it onto the bedside table each night and go to sleep feeling good about your next day's task? To that end, we've created steps to success. Each chapter details a new step toward your end goal: reaching and teaching to a fully aware and involved (evolved) teen self. These steps aspire to fortify your teaching tools to set the stage for the most receptive minds possible.

Steps to Success

Step 1: Understand and connect with the self behind the desk.

Step 2: Soften defenses to foster academic and personal growth.

Step 3: Provide tools for emotional management.

Step 4: Use cognitive understanding to awaken potentials.

Step 5: Consolidate the self in the social world.

Step 6: Support the physical self for optimal overall health.

Step 7: Create an environment that works for you.

Success for You

Although the main goal of this book is to reach and support each student's sense of self, that goal cannot be achieved unless you have continually checked in with your self and what feels right for you. Thus, within each chapter, you will find questions ("Check In With Your Self") that ask you to be very clear and real with yourself about who you are in relation to teaching and to the material presented. The book is based on the idea that a sense of self is the foundation to feeling successful, in school and out, but that sense of self is not exclusive to the student body. Your success also relies on your own self-reflection.

Teachers cannot begin to help and understand their students until they first understand themselves. How well do you understand yourself? How does the way you were raised affect your teaching style? Your ability to connect with students? Does it even matter? We suggest that it does. Immensely. And studies support this.

For instance, in 1994, a study found a positive relationship between teacher self-esteem and teacher classroom interaction. Students simply felt more comfortable, more connected, and more engaged with teachers who had higher self-esteem. The variables of age, years of teaching experience, and class enrollment showed no correlation (Lee & Hirschlein, 1994).

Self-esteem is a close cousin to one's sense of self. "Teachers with the clearest and most positive sense of self are in the best position to facilitate the development of high self-esteem in their students" (Lee & Hirschlein, 1994).

On a scale of 1 to 10, with 1 being low and 10 being high, please rate yourself:

_____My feelings of self-esteem

_____My stress level

_____My health

_____My productivity

_____My ability to connect with my students

If you follow the general findings, teachers who have a high self-esteem have lower stress levels, better health, productivity, and connections with their students.

You are the most significant person affecting your students' sense of self while they are at school. As such, please check in with your own. The better you feel about yourself, the more genuine you are and the more likely your students will connect with you. If your self-esteem is tenuous, we hope that through reading this book, it will become more solid by knowing who you are as a teacher who is striving to implement practices that promote your students' well-being on many levels.

CHAPTER SUMMARY

Check In With Your Self

The way I feel about myself (my container) has an impact on how I teach:

_____Not at all _____A little _____Somewhat _____Definitely

In addition to the "Check in With Your Self" section, each chapter will have intervention charts to help you flesh out appropriate interventions for challenging situations. Below is an example of the charts. Your work on these charts will begin in Chapter 2 where we take a detailed look into the development of the self.

Situation	Goal	Intervention
Describe a situation you hope to improve.	What do you hope to achieve with the student?	Which intervention in the chapter will you use?
Tanya spaces out during instruction time and makes careless mistakes. If I call her out, she is embarrassed.	*For Tanya to feel connected to the material and feel more comfortable in class.*	*I will try making eye contact with her and develop more of a connection. Getting to know her a bit may make her feel more comfortable.*

Outcome
List the time frame and overall impressions.
After a month, there has been an improvement in her attitude and her ability to pay attention. She is doing better overall.

The Development of the Self: Understand and Connect With the Self Behind the Desk

From studies conducted around the world, researchers have distilled a number of factors that enable such children of misfortune to beat the heavy odds against them. One factor turns out to be the presence in their lives of a charismatic adult—a person with whom they can identify and a person from whom they gather strength. And in a surprising number of cases, that person turns out to be a teacher.

—Segal (1988)

WHAT YOU WILL LEARN IN THIS CHAPTER

This chapter explores Step 1: Understand and connect with the self behind the desk. The main issues covered include:

- Early attachment and self development
- The role of shame

- The importance of connections
- Interventions for creating connections and teaching to the self

EARLY ATTACHMENT AND SELF DEVELOPMENT

Early attachments set the stage for our future successes, failures, personality traits, and indeed, our life capacities. After the parent or caregiver, it is the teacher who is the next adult primed to impact students' lives. Hence, connections are the first step in your journey to reach and teach to the self. The implications for the profound role that connections play will be revealed as you employ the interventions suggested throughout this book, beginning with the very earliest of connections: attachment.

John Bowlby (1988) discovered that as children grow, they *internalize* their relationship (connections) with attachment figures. If the attachment is secure, the baby will explore the world, separate (individuate), and mature in a healthy manner. If the attachment has problems, the baby will not feel secure to play, explore, and create meaningful social interactions to the best of his or her ability. Building on Bowlby's work, Mary Ainsworth went on to discover that *patterns of attachment have significant implications later in life in emotional maturity, peer relationships, and academic performance* (Ainsworth & Bell, 1970).

In 2005, building on Ainsworth's ideas, a group of researchers led by Dr. L. Alan Sroufe published *The Development of the Person: The Minnesota Study of Risk and Adaptation From Birth to Adulthood*, which studies the dynamics of developing children and their internal and external influences. During this investigation, the researchers watched and evaluated the interactions between caregivers and their 42-month-olds. As they followed these children into adulthood, they found that they could predict, with 77% accuracy, which of those children would eventually drop out of school. Those predictions were based on the quality of early attachments. Those with more secure attachments had a much greater chance at remaining in school. IQ and achievement test results did not influence the prediction (Sroufe, Egeland, Carlson, & Collins, 2005).

Let's take a closer look into the process of attachment.

Did you know? Psychiatric patients show far greater insecure attachments than the general population.

What Creates a "Secure Attachment"?

When we are young, we primarily look to our caregivers to validate our emotional state and thus, our sense of self. To illustrate this process, think about a mother and toddler at the park, sitting in the grass and enjoying the beautiful day. The mother empties the contents of her baby bag on the blanket and begins to play with the toddler. The toddler picks up toys, which ignites his imagination. As he plays, he checks in with his mom for approval. At first, she is engaged and smiles back at him, mirroring his sense of pride and accomplishment at his newly found toy car. "Zoom, zoom," says mom with a smile. *The toddler's sense of self is validated as mom mirrors or reflects the child's sense of joy and pride.* His self feels secure when his mother's experience matches his own—what he is feeling is reflected as being "right" and "okay." His mother is attuned, and he feels felt, understood, and validated. His sense of self is supported (versus negated). This is a positive step toward a secure attachment.

Suddenly, the mother's cell phone rings and she engages in a heated conversation. Thus, she responds less and less to the toddler's checking in with her (she becomes preoccupied with her own needs). Meanwhile, the toddler, delighted by his first "mirroring" success, brings over a stuffed dog and tries to make barking sounds. However, mom is now fully absorbed in the stress of the phone call, and she scowls and nudges him toward other toys. His delight is extinguished. *His self has not been validated.* He is confused. As his inner state is not reflected, conflict arises. He had put a "piece" of his happy and playful self out to his mother, and she reflected back a scowl—totally incongruent with his sense of self in the moment. He thus begins to doubt (subconsciously) the authenticity of his developing feelings and ultimately his true self. He begins to worry that something about his self is not worthy of connection.

When you interact with a person, you are putting a "piece" of yourself out "there" for that person to see. The reaction you get from the other person tells you how that "piece" of you was received. In the example above, the young boy's piece of himself was not well received, and as a result, his sense of self becomes insecure: *Why did that happen? What did I do wrong? Why is my mother not happy with me? Will she react the same way next time?* Our interactions with others, especially at a young age, mirror who we believe ourselves to be. Sometimes, as in the toy car example, the mirroring is congruent with our experience, and the result is that our sense of self is affirmed. Sometimes, however, the mirroring is not congruent, and our sense of self is not affirmed; it is denied (like the little boy with the stuffed dog), or worse.

Mirroring the sense of self happens every day in classrooms around the world. No matter the age, students can easily feel embarrassed or shamed when a teacher reflects an opposing self state. For instance, in art class, Caroline was feeling very proud of her ceramic piece until her teacher told her it was worthy only of the garbage can (this is, unfortunately, a true story).

In continuing with our example, the toddler, upset that his barking dog did not win praise or validation, now rummages through the pile and mommy's purse for something that may please mommy, only to find a pair of shiny scissors he's never seen. *Wow, this is amazing—so shiny and new.* His excitement overwhelms him. He is giddy with delight and rushes to mom to show off his new find with enthusiasm and glee. Mom, however, does not share his glee at the dangerous object in his hands. As such, she proceeds to rip the scissors from his hand, scold him, plop him down in a heap for a time out, and continues her phone call. *This response causes the child to feel shame for not only his actions, but for his self.*

Shame is a common, insidious feeling born from repeated misalignments in the early years. Knowing what causes shame, the symptoms of shame, and how to repair the damage will help students move beyond the debilitating side effects of shame.

The Development of Shame

Because of the complexities of life, most of us have mismatches from time to time. However, when a child repeatedly feels shameful, when he or she repeatedly puts a piece of himself or herself "out there" to find it rejected or scolded, the child will consolidate that feeling as part of who he or she is. A mismatch once in a while tells the self "I am generally okay." A mismatch on a more regular basis tells the self, "I cannot predict if my self will be well received." Feelings of unworthiness may develop from this thinking.

Thus, when a child feels repeated shame, the self may have difficulty absorbing love and/or positive interactions. Shame makes people feel unworthy of connection: *When I try to connect with others, I am often rejected. Something must be wrong with me. I am unworthy of attention or connection.* This creates insecurity (an insecure attachment), and the need for a false, protective self. The feeling that the self is flawed (or at least will not be well received) is the feeling of shame and the genesis of a false sense of self.

How could the mother have reacted differently? After all, the scissors *were* potentially dangerous to the child. Consider this response: The child presents the scissors to the mother. She mirrors excitement and awe. "Wow! So pretty! Let me see! Yes, I can see why you like these but they are not safe. Let's find something pretty and safe together . . . oh! Look at this shiny silver rattle! Here, have a look, my love." And with that, she hands the rattle to the toddler and places the scissors away. She has, with this response, validated the toddler's feelings, but also kept him safe by offering a more appropriate "toy."

Shame is different from guilt. Guilt says, "I did something wrong." Shame says, "There is something wrong with me." While guilt provides a sense of morality and may prove helpful to right a wrong, shame splinters the self and steals a part of the innocence and playfulness so inherent of youth. Everyone benefits when shame is not given a voice in the classroom.

TRUE SELF VERSUS FALSE SELF: THE BATTLE BEGINS

D. W. Winnicott (1960), a psychoanalyst who focused on object-relations theory, developed the idea of the true self and the false self. Self states develop in the early years, as demonstrated above, and continue to show up in your classroom, which is why an understanding of them will enable the capacity for appropriate intervention, ultimate connection, and more life success. The *true* self appears when a child feels connected, supported, and therefore safe to express himself spontaneously. His real feelings, needs, and desires are in tune with the caregiver. The child *feels accepted by and connected to the parent* when expressing ideas and emotions (*zoom, zoom goes the car*), and thus, feeling secure in himself, he will be more likely to be open and engaged in your classroom.

However, mismatches between parent and child during the early years can lead toward the opposite state: an unhealthy *false* self. People who have developed a false self typically have greater difficulties connecting with others and forming meaningful relationships. This is because the core of the person feels hollow, at the very least—flooded with insecurities and defenses. The false self develops because the child has a natural need for the caretaker's acceptance and affection, but the need has not been fulfilled.

Check In With Your Self

Can you tell the difference between feeling guilty and feeling shameful? Have you felt either? How did you react?

How do you relate to or comfort a student who feels shame?

A child with a false self will develop strategies to protect himself or herself from the world. *I do not want you to see that I am flawed. I don't want to experience the pain of rejection.* With shame at his or her core and a false self directing his or her life, a child can make many decisions that will cause him or her and others pain. Self-doubt, depression, and unhappiness may develop. A false self manifests in many forms, from bullying to acting out and to self-harm: each of these are defenses from shame and from other insecure feelings related to the self.

The Birth of Defenses

Defenses are strategies (detailed in Chapter 3) that protect a person's sense of self. Defenses are what you may see in your classroom when you are unable to connect with a child no matter how you approach him. As you saw in our toddler story, children *internalize* their experiences. At all times, they are learning about themselves from the world around them and they take the majority of their cues from their caregivers and significant others. Thus, when a parent tells a child she is an "idiot," she will tend to internalize this and believe it as true, rather than to see it as a statement made by a very frustrated person. In defense, the child will adapt methods and behaviors that hide that terrible self-perception (*I am an idiot*) from others, and react to situations in ways that ward off further hurt (*I will not let you get close enough, lest you see that I am an idiot.*) Ultimately, simply put, *our perceptions about who we are can become inaccurate from a very early age (an unhealthy false self develops), and we will use defenses to hide those (inaccurate) self-perceptions.*

A Word of Caution

We are not suggesting that all emotional difficulties in your classroom are the sole fault of a parent or are all a result of neglect. It takes nature, nurture, fate, and sometimes an unexpected twist to create our unique personalities. Exploring unmet needs is not a blame game; it simply helps to construct better tools for the future.

Fortunately, the self is still developing, and methods (which we describe throughout the book) can be quite successful in softening the defenses and developing the true self. *Developing the true, authentic, aware self is a critical contributing factor to mental health.* The first step toward softening defenses begins with creating connections.

MAKING CONNECTIONS

The Power of Touch

Touch is one of the most powerful and precise ways humans connect with each other. Even small gestures can greatly influence how we feel about one another. For instance, the students who were touched by librarians while returning their library cards rated the librarian and the library more favorably. However, in today's litigious society, many of us have become reluctant to touch students, leaving our innate humanity at home. But if you stick to the safety zones (shoulders, backs, arms—high fives, pats on the back) you can greatly increase the feelings of connection your students have with you (Chillot, 2013).

Human connection is just as important as nourishment for brain and physical development and ultimate survival. Indeed, we are neurobiologically and physiologically wired for connection: From the earliest moments of our lives, we rely on social interactions for the healthy development of our moral, civic, and psychological self. Babies who are not held (or nurtured, loved, or spoken to) fail to thrive: They develop neurological problems, show cognitive decline, and even die (Perry, 2006). These early attachments may set the stage for lifelong social interactions, but they do not need to define us. Yes, they play a critical role in shaping our personality, but as brain research (Chapter 5) and psychological practices teach us, we have ample opportunity to change our brains and work out the nuances of our (sometimes) troubled past. Educators have a profound capacity to create positive and authentic connections that can repair the self.

Martin Seligman, one of the leading researchers and innovators in positive psychology, points out the critical role positive relationships play in overall well-being. In his book *Flourish* (2011), Seligman cites positive relationships as one of the five core elements for leading a life full of meaning and well-being. He writes,

Very little that is positive is solitary. When was the last time you laughed uproariously? The last time you felt indescribable joy? The last time you sensed profound meaning and purpose? . . . Even without knowing the particulars of these high points of your life, I know their form: all of them took place around other people. (p. 20)

Feeling connected to other people brings meaning to our lives. People who find themselves facing death unexpectedly, such as in an imminent plane crash, don't call to work to prep coworkers on the agenda items they will miss the next day. They call home. They call loved ones. They cry for the lost time with those with whom they are connected.

We thrive on connection, while we suffer from disconnection—as demonstrated in our early attachment example of the mother and child at the park. But disconnection does not just create problems in the formative years. Think of the stories you have heard about mass shootings by a lone gunman in the United States (Columbine, Virginia Tech, Colorado movie theatre massacre, Newtown, CT). The one defining characteristic that all of the gunmen shared: social disconnect. In fact, loneliness is a key contributor and indicator of depression (Cacioppo & William, 2008). *Disconnection damages the self. Connection builds the self.*

As indicated by the Sroufe et al. (2005) study mentioned earlier in this chapter, the need for connection during childhood development is critical because early attachments best predicted school dropout rates. Indeed, the students who eventually graduated (who were observed as having positive early attachments with their caregivers) reported that they found building and maintaining relationships with their peers and with adults easy. They also felt connected to at least one "special" teacher. The students who dropped out, and who were observed as having poor attachments with their caregivers, reported that they were unable to make connections with adults and that they did not feel a connection to any "special" teachers. Early attachment quality does not have to be the crystal ball that Sroufe and his colleagues found. Positive connections have tremendous power throughout our lifetimes. As teachers with young, developing, curious minds in front of you, you have a chance to intervene and catch a student before he or she falls. You always have a chance to make connections.

Connection promotes growth—socially, physically, emotionally, and cognitively. If any member of your school community feels alienated, learning and achievement will be compromised while anger and resentment will become dominant roadblocks to success. If you want your students to connect with and retain your material, first connect with their selves.

Without first developing an authentic, trusted, two-way connection with your students, all of the strategies and interventions we suggest will go out the

---

Check In With Your Self

How do you form connections with others? Is it easy or difficult? How does your upbringing, culture, traditions, personality style, etc. influence your ability to connect with others?

*window. And those guarded and heavily defended students? Their windows are wide open, complete with a fan to help shoo your attempts at false connections right on out. Your students need to **feel** that they can trust you.*

Interventions to Promote Connections

> For authentic connection to develop, you may need to let go of who you think you should be in order to be who you are (Brown, 2011). This is one reason why self-reflective questions are sprinkled throughout the book.

Throughout this book, you will be offered many strategies (we refer to them as interventions) to help you reach and teach to the self: to polish and rebuild those inner containers. The purpose of these interventions is to help you connect with students so that you can help them begin to identify with their true self. The true self is found deep inside the multilayers of self-preservation (unhealthy false self beliefs, defenses, and so forth). The interventions provided throughout this book will help you carefully fold back a few of those layers, reaching the potential inside your students while also making your classroom climate feel safe.

Intervention 2.1: Come Alongside Your Students—Align With the True Self

Instead of coming *at* a student, think about coming "alongside" him. Pretend you are helping him to navigate a car. If you stand in front of him and point directions, he will always feel like you are in the way, even though you are giving good directions. If you sit in the car next to him and utter the same directions, he is much more likely to enjoy the ride (Stiffleman, 2010).

A good technique for achieving this is to consider a few reasons why a student is acting a certain way. For instance, if a child is misbehaving in your classroom, consider some reasons why, according to *her world view,* she might "do that"—even if your mind is screaming, "She shouldn't do that!" Then, once you have a kernel of understanding for why your student might be behaving a certain way, get in the passenger seat and go for a ride with her. Ask her how she is feeling. Ask her what she wants. Ask her what you can do to help her get there. Stand next to her with the problem rather than in front of her.

> *Come alongside your students* is not just metaphorical: When discussing a problem with them, sit next to them rather than across from them. This creates the feeling that you are working with them and thus mitigates the power imbalance. Their self will feel supported rather than confronted. In essence, don't sit on the hood of the car to give directions, sit in the passenger seat.

Example 2.1: Come Alongside Your Students

Jeremy is constantly talking during your class. You have asked him time and again to be quiet and even sent him to the principal on several occasions. You feel he "should" be quiet during class as it is disruptive and disrespectful to the other students, as well as to you. But, nothing seems to work with Jeremy.

Now think to yourself, *What are two good reasons Jeremy wants to talk in my class?* You might eventually think, *Well, he gets a lot of attention from others when he talks,* and, *He gets a lot of attention from me when he talks.* You might even then come up with, *Well, he's in middle school and talking with your friends is really fun, perhaps more fun than listening to a lesson.*

Note: we are not saying these reasons are more important than the reasons you have for wanting him to stay quiet. But understanding his perspective, seeing the world through his windshield, may help you to soften your attitude toward him.

Then, try talking to him privately. Ask him what it's like for him to be in your classroom with his friends. Ask him how he feels when you ask him to be quiet. Ask him if he feels like he has enough time to talk with his friends outside your classroom. Finally, ask him if there is something you can do to help him be quiet in the classroom. Help him find a solution. Help him navigate the road.

Intervention 2.2: Reflect Who You Know the Student Is Capable of Being

Reflect to the student who he truly is capable of being, not a fragmented self that is burdened with shame and held together by defenses. Believe in your students when they don't believe in themselves. When a student whines to you, "It's just too hard, I'll never get it," then affirm your belief in him that he can "get it" by saying, "Leor, I have faith in you. You will get it. You can do it." Support your students not just in their academic struggles but in their social and behavioral struggles as well:

"Jeanette, I know you tell me that you can't help it when you speak out of turn, but I know you. I know you can control yourself. I see you in other classes. You have the ability to do it."

Sometimes a feeling of inadequacy may overcome a student, and you will need to make a repair that helps the student incorporate a positive self-concept rather than digest the negative one just displayed. For example, to a highly agitated student, you might say, "Sitting still is challenging sometimes, I know. But I've seen you do it many times before. Now would be a great time. Thank you." Your eyes, ears, and subsequent interpretation of your students' evolving selves serve as a palpable reflection to them. Make that reflection positive.

Teacher Illustration 2.2:
Reflecting the Potential Inside

Jennifer Larson, MA Curriculum and Instruction, Faculty, Far Hills Country Day School, Far Hills, NJ

Mathematics is a subject that can cause some anxiety in students (and in adults). I have a young man in my seventh-grade prealgebra class who has incredible math anxiety. If there is a scheduled assessment, he will walk in the door and announce, "I'm going to fail this" and he believes it. All year, we have been working on overcoming this anxiety. Traditionally, math is taught with writing as the main tool for instruction; students are involved in copying notes, practicing skills, and completing written assessments; however, some students need to both process and express their thinking verbally. In my classroom, we do a great deal of communicating mathematics during discussions where students can ask and answer questions with their peers and with me as the facilitator. With this particular young man, he'll often ask a question, and when he's verbalized the question, he is able to answer it himself. We have used this insight to help create positive self-talk during our classes and assessments. Although he is nervous, he is beginning to believe in himself more. We're building his confidence and working on creating tools to use both in and out of the classroom. He doesn't shut down anymore when he doesn't understand something, and he keeps asking questions, verbalizing his thinking. The more he verbalizes, the more he understands. I am confident that he will be successful, and he hasn't ever failed a test!

> **Check In With Your Self**
>
> Do you find yourself labeling students as troublemakers, party animals, or worse? Why? Why are they putting out those messages for the world, and how can you mirror back an image that protects the self and nourishes a more "acceptable" self?

Intervention 2.3: Teach and Promote the Five-Finger Rule

Check in with your students, especially those you feel could be socially at risk, to make sure they have a few individuals to whom they feel they can turn for help and guidance. Promote connections and make your students aware that having a support system is beneficial to their health. We advocate the five-finger rule—five trusted people, each from a different sector of the students' lives: one from school, one from community, one from home, one from extended family, and one from their place of worship or from an organization with which they feel close (such as a sport club). Can your students name a person from your school with whom they feel connected? Can your faculty get together and make sure every student has a connection with someone? Below is an example of how to do so.

Intervention 2.4: Index Cards

Create index cards representing each student in an effort to be sure that all students feel a sense of connection with at least one adult in school. This idea was presented at the National School Climate Center's 2010 summer conference: Have your school personnel create an index card that represents each student you are serving. Provide colored sticker dots to all the personnel. If a person feels a connection to a student on the index card, he or she is to place a dot on that card. A connection can be defined as a daily high five, a knowing glance of concern each week, a private talk every once in a while when the student needs advice or an ear, a hello each day in the hallway using the student's name. Once all the teachers, cafeteria workers, crossing guards, janitorial staff, and the rest of the school personnel have had a chance to contribute their dots, take a look at the index cards. The students with no dots attached are at the greatest risk for dropping out. Immediately develop a strategy for making a connection with those students.

Intervention 2.5: Support Student Efforts to Connect

Some students feel so out of tune with others because of damaged early attachments that they need a lot of help making connections or recognizing their value. Some children are naturally shyer than others, so we are not suggesting that every child needs to run a popularity contest. What we are suggesting is that social connection is vital, no matter how big or small.

Encourage naturally shyer or generally more reluctant students to reach out; pair them with others and affirm their social selves: "You did well on the group project today. I appreciate the leadership skills you demonstrated." Additionally, subtle remarks such as, "Your support of the soccer game today was really appreciated," can help a reclusive student feel seen and appreciated. By reinforcing positive social skills, you help them incorporate another aspect of themselves through your eyes, and you make connections. To the student who has specific trouble getting along with others, you may suggest, "Going out of your way to do something really nice for someone else can feel strange if no one ever did it for you." This is an example of an intervention discussed more fully in Chapter 3. It demonstrates how expressing a student's perhaps-yet-unknown feeling can help him or her to reflect upon his or her self and the behavioral options that are available to him or her.

Teacher Illustration 2.5: Connecting With Cathy

Amy Smith, English Teacher, Ramapo High School, Franklin Lakes, NJ

Cathy, a tenth-grade girl in my English class was rather shy, and she didn't seem to have many friends. By choice, she sat in the first seat of the middle row and would often drop in after school just to "chat." I was the advisor of the school newspaper, and many times, I had to cut our chats short or was just leaving when she entered my classroom. One afternoon, Cathy told me that she had lost the sight in her left eye and that she was also losing the sight in her right eye and that it would only be a matter of time before she would be blind. Shocked, I asked her all about the problem. I was so upset that I called my own ophthalmologist that afternoon and asked if he would please see this student. Based on what she had told me that afternoon, I didn't think Cathy had the right diagnosis or treatment, as she said her doctor told her there was nothing he could do. That night, I called my student's home and asked her if it would be all right if my doctor saw Cathy. Her mother was stunned and told me there was absolutely nothing wrong with her daughter's eyesight. I was shocked and wondered what would make a child do something like that, but I soon came to understand why.

The next morning, Cathy told me that she really liked talking to me but that I always seemed so busy and didn't have time for her. So, she manufactured the eyesight story thinking that I would spend more time with her if I felt sorry for her. I explained to her that it was true: I was very busy but told her that we could spend much more time together if she would take a position on the newspaper staff. She was elated with the idea, and she became a reporter. We spent quite a bit of time together in a productive way that year. She felt better about herself and spent a lot of quality time with her peers and me.

Intervention 2.6: Share Your Self!

> "Relationships are the agents of change and the most powerful therapy is human love" (Perry, 2006, p. 230).

As you put your self out there for students to see and contemplate, they will naturally determine if the environment is safe for them to do the same—to connect with you. Clearly, boundaries remain intact, not all aspects of your personal life need to be written on the chalkboard, but do consider sharing appropriately with your students. Emulate that your self is safe in the room, so their selves are too.

CHAPTER SUMMARY

As we explore the many ways to create connections in the following chapters, please remember the true self of the child sitting behind the desk. Behind that gruff (or guarded) exterior is a self that yearns to be seen. Who will you choose to see?

Check In With Your Self

I think that my childhood experiences, including the way I was raised, influence me as a teacher.

____ Not so much ____ Sometimes ____ Most of the time ____ Of course, all the time

I think that thinking about how I relate to my students and connect with them has an impact on my ability to teach my students.

____ Not so much ____ Sometimes ____ Most of the time ____ Of course, all the time

---

Please use the intervention chart below by answering the prompts and applying some of the interventions learned in this chapter.

Interventions

Come alongside a student—align with the true self

Reflect who you know the student is capable of being

Teach and promote the five-finger rule

Index cards

Support student efforts to connect

Share your self

Activity: Connect and Support the Developing Self

Situation	Goal	Intervention
Describe a situation you hope to improve. *I am baffled about how to connect with Emeril. He is angry with the world and with me.*	What do you hope to achieve with the student? *I would like Emeril to be less angry with me and thus more engaged in class.*	Which intervention in the chapter will you use? *Reflect who he is capable of being.* *Come alongside him.*

Outcome
List the time frame and overall impressions. *After 5 weeks of commenting on his positive qualities, Emeril finally cracked a smile with me over his "forgotten" homework. After concurring that owning a pit bull has its ups and downs, I tried to gently come alongside by suggesting that the challenges of homework completion is something he can get through. I think maybe for once he didn't feel attacked. Homework was turned in the next day.*

Now construct a chart from your experience.

The Unaware Emotional Self: Soften Defenses to Foster Academic and Personal Growth

People who lack emotion don't lead well-planned logical lives in the manner of coolly rational Mr. Spocks. They lead foolish lives. In the extreme cases, they become sociopaths, untroubled by barbarism and unable to feel other people's pain.

—Brooks (2011, p. 19)

WHAT YOU WILL LEARN IN THIS CHAPTER

This chapter covers Step 2: Soften defenses to foster academic and personal growth. After reading this chapter, you will know

- The purpose of defenses
- How defenses develop
- How defenses inhibit optimal learning
- Common defensive patterns and how they may manifest in the classroom
- Interventions that build the self

THE PURPOSE OF DEFENSES

Emotional well-being is key to an optimal learning environment (Brackett, Reyes, Rivers, Elbertson, & Salovey, 2011; Combs, 1991; Elias & Zins, 2006). However, subconscious emotions can impede progress toward this end. Subconscious emotions are those of which we are not fully aware, and yet, nevertheless, drive our behaviors. Some do so positively (we write a letter to a friend "just because"), while other subconscious emotions affect us negatively (we behave in ways that hinder showing our authentic selves to the world). *We call these psychic obstacles to optimal learning and behavior* **defenses** (Freud, 1979).

Defenses are built to safeguard the self from overwhelming negative and difficult emotions. As such, they serve an important function: to preserve the self, and we are all for self-preservation! However, a cost is involved when the defenses continue into adulthood: they limit potential connections and personal growth. For this reason, addressing them early is of great benefit to you and your students.

A defensive nature can be tricky as it is usually *outside of a student's conscious awareness.* You are not expected to "fix" or break down the defenses. Think of them like a padlock on that inner container that curtails your efforts at repair and connection while keeping a student's negative self-perceptions "locked in." We simply need to find the right combination to unlock the defenses. This chapter will walk you through their development, list some common defenses, and show you what they may look like in your classroom. The interventions listed later in this chapter will help you soften those defenses, thereby increasing the chances of a positive connection with your students (and thus decreasing the likelihood of dropout and failure) (Sroufe, Egeland, Carlson, & Collins, 2005).

THE DEVELOPMENT OF DEFENSES AND HOW THEY INHIBIT OPTIMAL LEARNING

> Upon completion of *David,* Michelangelo remarked that *David* was always within the block of stone; it needed merely the tools, imagination, and a careful chipping away of the stone to reveal the potential inside.

Each stage of a child's development makes demands on the caregiver to meet specific growth and emotional needs. Sometimes they are met, and sometimes they are not. When those needs are *not met,* the child's psyche adapts by forming a network of defenses for self-preservation: The defenses protect the self from uncomfortable feelings such as *I am not loved, needed, or wanted; I am worthless.* Defenses are built to ward off both that original hurt and any further painful interactions.

The child who is disruptive, checked out, distant, overly sensitive, flippant, or uncaring is the child who is showing you defenses. For example, the child who fears rejection may think, *Don't come near me. I'm already in pain. I can feel the ultimate rejection so I will reject you first to save face.* But beneath the defensive veneer lies a unique person with much to offer the world. When we teach to the self, we are striving to reach and heal the injured self beneath the defensive veneer—to "see" the child *inside* and empower him or her with more confidence and help the child to let go of his or her distorted self-perceptions.

However, to discuss the defenses logically with a student is counterintuitive because defenses are usually buried deep in the subconscious. But the importance of recognizing and dealing with this subconscious manifestation of an unmet childhood need cannot be ignored. When you can intervene by supporting the self, optimal learning can be restored. We will provide a few tools for you to help soften those defensive blocks so connections with your students become possible.

Prejudice Pit Stop

Think of a person you know who has a particular prejudice. Is this person aware of the prejudice, or does he truly believe that what he feels is the truth? Most likely, he will distort facts and events to maintain his prejudice. He will make assumptions, generalize, and even name call to solidify his case. This is just like the damaged self—children who have been prejudiced to believe that something is wrong with them will set up a host of defenses to keep that belief intact (Padesky, 1990).

COMMON DEFENSE MECHANISMS AND HOW THEY MAY MANIFEST IN THE CLASSROOM

A character or personality disorder has the potential to create far greater social consequences than the actions of someone suffering from a psychotic break. For example, a person with narcissistic personality disorder, a disorder that entangles the self with defenses (think Hitler, Qaddafi, etc.), can do more widespread damage than a person with paranoid schizophrenia. Furthermore, the symptoms are easier to spot with a psychosis than with a character disorder. This is why a program that focuses on developing the self can have tremendous repercussions on society at large.

Below is a list of a few common defenses and how they may surface in your classrooms. Understanding and being aware of defenses will help you change your reactions to challenging behaviors to more positive and effective responses. Your realization that the behavior in your classroom is ultimately a defense developed early in life to protect the self from injury is a shift in consciousness that supports student self development. *Defenses are a fear-based reaction: Try to remind yourself that through a defense mechanism, as frustrating as it can be, a teen is really saying (albeit subconsciously), "Please don't hurt me."* With this perspective, learning about defenses can help you to support the self and create change. The defense mechanisms listed below are in order from the most primitive (early self-injuries) to more adaptive coping mechanisms.

1.   *Denial: Repression at its extreme whereby a student will deny the existence of a feeling or problem because the resulting emotion would be unbearable.* Denial is commonly found in people who suffer from addiction and may report, "I don't have a drinking problem." At school, a failing student may say, "Grades don't mean anything to me. I didn't even try that hard on the test!" Expressing genuine emotion would make this student feel weak or stupid. Students rarely seek help for painful emotional situations that derail them from life success. Instead, they obsessively deny them, "Min would never cheat on me; everyone saying so is wrong."

2.   *Regression: A return to an earlier stage of development.* In your class, for example, you may have a teen who cries easily, has temper tantrums, or even wets his pants. This behavior is a sign of emotional chaos. Connection, empathy, and likely counseling intervention are warranted to help the student manage.

3.   *Acting Out: Means to act in a way that expresses an unconscious wish without awareness of the emotion driving the behavior.* You may see this in your classroom when students act out in order not to learn. Perhaps the material subconsciously makes them feel dumb so they disrupt the class to defend against the feelings induced by the material. Bullying is an example of acting out.

4.   *Dissociation: Disconnecting from the real world in order to preserve the self.* For example, children who have been traumatized may dissociate, seeming as though they are daydreaming, and you need to bring them back. Either they have been repeatedly abused (for instance, verbally assaulted so much that they literally learn how to "tune out"), or they have witnessed abuse and have learned how to shut out their worlds. Intervene by providing a safe atmosphere and building an authentic connection with the student.

5. *Projection: Disowning feelings and attributing them to someone else.* This defense mechanism can be seen when a student might say, "You're the one with the problem. I'm totally fine!" Or, "You're the bully, not me!" Projection comes from a lack of insight. Hence, a program that increases self-awareness helps with this (and other defenses).

6. *Repression: Keeping upsetting events, thoughts, and feelings buried in the subconscious.* If a child represses her abuse, she will not consciously remember it; her mind will inhibit the memory from conscious recall. However, the feelings associated with it may *not be entirely inhibited,* and subsequently, those feelings may show up in your classroom. For example, 1 in 12 young people self-harm (Kelland, 2011). This behavior is an example of repressed emotions seeking discharge through the pain of cutting, burning, or other life-threatening risks. When students repress thoughts and feelings, they manifest in ways that hinder self-success.

7. *Displacement: Aggression or impulses redirected to another less psychically risky target.* A student may be angry toward a parent but directs his anger at a teacher because anger at the parent would risk self-injurious retaliation. The teacher is a less risky target. A student may fight with another student for a completely unrelated reason when, in fact, she was angry and striking out because her father had just been diagnosed with cancer.

8. *Rationalization: Explaining an unacceptable thought, action, or response in a rational or logical way, often without accepting the true reason— likely the unconscious reason.* After a fight in the cafeteria, the aggressor might say, "I didn't tell on him because I knew you wouldn't believe me, so I punched him and he deserved it." This is an example of a student justifying why hitting his classmate, who stole his lunch money, was fair. This student feels the need to explain why violence was his choice; admitting that he did something "wrong," or that he was a victim of bullying, would make him feel too vulnerable.

9. *Sublimation: Converting unacceptable impulses, thoughts, or feelings into more acceptable ones.* A girl who is bullied may feel targeted and excluded, but instead of taking it out on someone and creating another "victim," she becomes an amazing athlete, channeling her anger onto the sports field.

> **Check In With Your Self**
>
> Do your emotions *hinder* your performance as an educator *or help* you relate to what others may be feeling? Can you name one defense you may have? Of all the defenses listed, which ones do you relate to the most? Why? Which do you see among your students?

Note: We are not suggesting that you break down a defense by exposing it outright (defenses serve a purpose: to protect the self from further hurt). Without those defenses, a child would be at risk for more severe psychiatric or antisocial behaviors. *We are suggesting that by teaching to the self you begin to strengthen the psyche and unleash the hold that these defenses have had on students' potential or, at the very least, help students move from one level to the next, discarding old defensive armors for more rational and higher-level ones.* (If you believe a student is developing more severe patterns of behavior and poses a risk to himself/herself or others, the school counselor should be notified.)

Thus far, we have explained why we build defenses and listed many common defenses while providing examples for how they manifest in the classroom and impede optimal learning. In the next section, we cover how to manage those defenses and help the student rebuild his or her sense of self, so he or she may return to the important task of learning and finding more success in personal, relational, and academic pursuits.

HOW TO MANAGE DEFENSES THROUGH INTERVENTIONS THAT BUILD THE SELF

Ultimately, the self is always looking for connections, but the self must feel safe in order to lower its defenses and allow those connections to happen. When that occurs, you will be helping to shine a student's container rather than fill it with additional negative self-perceptions and experiences. The interventions listed in this section will help you create those feelings of security.

Interventions such as *object-oriented language, validation, mirroring, scaffolding,* and *listening for intent* are used to empower the self by safely and carefully providing a language to the emotions hindering performance. This way, you can reduce the power a defense has over your student and, subsequently, over your classroom. Below you will find an explanation of these techniques and classroom examples.

A Word of Caution About Our Intentions!

As an educator, please do not be deluded that we are suggesting you come to a child's emotional rescue. You are not being called upon to magically supply all the love, attention, validation, or acceptance that a student has missed along his or her journey. An attempt to do so may frustrate the student and leave him or her wondering, *Just who do you think you are barging in on my personal stuff? Get lost!*

Instead, what we are suggesting is that you develop connections with your student; support her true, wonderful self; help him to feel heard; soften a few defenses when possible; and promote self- and emotional awareness.

Teaching to the self creates valuable connections and is actually a natural extension of all human contact and the desire to teach. An example of one teacher's experience: "One day a week, I make myself available to my students after school. This is beyond my usual extra help hours. The students know they can come talk to me about anything. Over the years, I have found that the students who come in to talk—about anything they want—end up improving in my class, both academically and in their behavior" (Erin Filner, Seventh-Grade Social Studies Teacher, Bedford, NY).

Intervention 3.1: Object-Oriented Language

In psychological terms, the *object* is something separate from the self, whereas the *ego* is the self. So, when we make repairs to the self, it is sometimes easier on the psyche when we use "other" things (objects) or people as examples rather than putting the self on the hot seat. (The ego loves flattery but hates the hot seat.) When a topic is emotionally charged or feels too personal for a student, the student's ability to stay focused on the material can diminish, and he may even act out (a defense) his unmanageable feelings, disturbing your classroom. A subtle shift in focus from the ego (the student) toward an object (such as a character in a book) distances the emotions from the student making those emotions less intrusive and thus more manageable. It takes the ego off the hot seat and allows a student to work through the emotions (and thus "deal" with them) at a more comfortable level.

Example 3.1: Using Object-Oriented Examples and Language

To help her class deal with a schoolyard brawl turned bloody and violent, one tenth-grade English teacher referred to a recent reading of *The Outsiders* and asked the students to reflect on how the main character (Ponyboy) may have felt in the situation; how the onlookers (both the Greasers and Socs) may have felt; and how the change maker (Cherry) may have felt. Once the emotions were acknowledged in regard to the story (the story thus becoming the object), processing the traumatic scene of the schoolyard fight became easier for her students because the relevant emotions had found a safe and acceptable avenue of release. This intervention of using an object-oriented means (the character of a book or historical figure) helps students reflect upon their emotions in a less personal and thus safer way. Simply expressing the pent-up emotions, even in regards to a character, helps discharge those emotions so learning has more space in the mind.

Teacher Illustration 3.1: Object-Oriented Intervention

Dr. Thomas Gorman, Principal, Ridgewood High School, NJ

Role playing has been successful in allowing our students to address challenging topics in a safer, less personal way. Last year, we brought in some NY Giants players as part of their community outreach program to speak to the eighth- and ninth-grade class. They role-played scenarios that students encounter—sex, drugs, parties, etc. Each skit set up a possible social situation. After the skits, the class of students was asked to comment on the roles of the actors and the scenarios. The students liked participating because they were able to talk about the actors and scenes, not about themselves. They all nervously laughed at many of the scenes, but many had been exposed to similar types of peer pressures and felt empowered learning from the skits.

Intervention 3.2: Validation

We can help teens by simply listening to them, validating their need to express who they are without threat of attack or criticism (especially as so much of what they have to say is often judged or contradicted by others). Validation means recognizing the value of a feeling—that it is real. *We don't have to agree with a feeling,* but acknowledging that a feeling is real to a student helps authenticate his or her experience. The self needs expression and validation in order to create and solidify itself. Validating says to a student "I hear you" (not "I agree with you"), and feeling heard allows the self to feel connected and safe.

Example 3.2: Validation

Ahmed forgot to do his homework again this week, and according to the rules in your classroom, he has to stay in during lunchtime to complete it. During that time, he is surly and disrespectful to you, commenting, "This is so stupid, a total waste of my time." (He is acting out.) You could defend your decision and comment on how being in at lunchtime is also a waste of *your* time, but recognizing and connecting with Ahmed's sense of self and his feelings will serve you (and him!) better. Try: "It seems that you would rather be with your friends having fun than feeling like you are wasting your time doing a homework assignment, especially one in which you find no value." This acknowledges to Ahmed's self that his feelings are real and somewhat understandable. You are validating his experience for him—putting words to his feelings. Ahmed may have rarely felt validated by, or connected to, anyone. Initial attempts may be thwarted, but keep at it. You are chipping away at the defenses to reach the potential found inside. Once you have *connected* with him in this way, his defenses are more likely to soften and he may be more open to creating homework strategies that will keep him from missing further lunches with his friends. Don't become frustrated if his defenses don't soften right away. Remember, his defenses have been created over his lifetime. Like a frozen stick of butter, they may take time to thaw to a point where they are not so rigid. Over time, patience and validation will help Ahmed express his more subconscious feelings that are keeping him from attending to the work at hand.

Intervention 3.3: Mirroring

Mirroring is used when the student is *unaware of his or her feelings* and needs help bringing them to consciousness. When you mirror, you act as a reflection to the subconscious *emotions* and enable their safe expression. This works well in cases of frustration or anger, as uncovering those emotions can often help the student handle them more effectively. (This would not, however, be the best technique for someone who is feeling like a loser, because indeed, mirroring that feeling would be hurtful.) Mirroring does the following:

- It validates and gives voice to the unconscious emotions that are truly at work.
- It shows empathy; you can relate.
- It empowers the self to resolve the situation.

Example 3.3: Mirroring

Max, a high school student with emotional issues, confides in you that he hates his math teacher. You happen to know that the math teacher really likes Max and that Max has had a difficult childhood, filled with abandonment, abuse, and neglect. Max comes to you one day and says,

"I hate Mr. Shapiro. He always criticizes me and rejects all my attempts at solving problems. He won't call on me, ignores me, and hates me!" Notice that Max never says how this makes him feel. Thus, mirroring the emotions behind these outbursts familiarizes Max with their emotional context: "Sounds like it really hurts when people are neglectful of your needs." By mirroring and giving voice to his subconscious emotions, you bring them to consciousness so strategies can be developed. Max may continue to cite examples of Mr. Shapiro's disregard for him, but when he does, try to uncover the underlying emotion by mirroring what is really going on (*how frustrating to not be called on when you know the answers*) and promote a solution-driven discussion with a question such as "How can you learn to manage situations in which you feel so frustrated?" This conversation could continue and prove to be rather effective in helping Max discuss his feelings and the early life situations that hurt him. (If appropriate, the school counselor may need to be contacted to bring this to the next level—making connections between how Mr. Shapiro makes him feel and how his parents made him feel. Indeed, this latter idea is a sophisticated intervention, but well worth consideration.)

Intervention 3.4: Scaffolding

Kids at all ages need to feel supported, emotionally, cognitively, and even physically at times as they move from one level of functioning to the next. Scaffolding means giving students just enough support to accomplish a task until they can accomplish it on their own, at which point the scaffolding (help) is removed and reinforced at the next higher level. Scaffolding means you are there to "hold them up" but not "carry them through." They must solve problems by themselves to grow. Proper scaffolding allows them to struggle with the challenge but not fail from frustration, all the while creating more connections with you. Scaffolding is inherently used with almost all students but may be particularly helpful with students who resist learning and cry out, "I can't do it!" Scaffolding makes the self feel safe enough to take the next step in learning.

Example 3.4: Scaffolding

Paulina brings her algebra homework to your desk and says, "This makes no sense. I hate these problems." Clearly frustrated, she sounds desperate to relieve herself of the work. You could, very easily, do the problem in front of her to demonstrate how it is done, but how will that polish her container? You realize that Paulina is having a problem with conceptualizing a as a number value. As such, you take your paper clip holder and leave only six paper clips in it. You then get Paulina to see that the holder itself can represent six paper clips. Paulina nods her head in under-standing. You then turn back to the problem she has presented you and prompt, "Perhaps you can see *a* like the paper clip holder, it represents a number. So let's try it again." Sitting next to her, you let her attempt the problem again. She struggles a bit, but you encourage her efforts, and in the end, she gets it, the smile on her face full of pride. You supported her with just enough help to move her to the next level (and scrape off a bit of barnacle—self-doubt—in the process).

Teacher Illustration 3.4: Scaffolding Intervention

Dr. Thomas Gorman, Principal, Ridgewood High School, NJ

History research papers (between five to 10 pages in length depending on the class level and age) were assigned in multiple steps in order to scaf-fold the students along the way. Each step was worth 10 or so points, which eventually totaled 100 points. So, the thesis statement was worth 10 points, the notes were worth 10 points, the annotated bibliography was worth 10 points, and so on. The final draft was only worth 10 points because the rough draft and all the other steps had already been read and handed back with comments.

This approach allowed for greater student success as opposed to assigning the research paper with a final due date and no interventions beforehand. Working with the student on the thesis, getting her argument that she wanted to defend correctly worded, led to future success. We worked and reworked the statement until it was perfect, and then she could move on to the next step. Each step brought success and broke down a seemingly overwhelming task into manageable steps while setting the stage for potential connections.

Intervention 3.5: Managing a Group Resistance

A *group* resistance refers to "the class . . . making known its will to resist being a mature class. This is indeed a powerful resistance and must be dealt with on a priority basis" (Kirman, 1977, p. 69). The resistance to learning could stem from boredom, the latest gossip, or a more pervasive anger permeating the group. Managing the resistance entails, first, recog-nizing that your classroom is full of students who have very real thoughts and feelings in reaction to different situations inside and outside of your classroom and, second, addressing those concerns to clear the air. Although your main focus at school may be academics, that priority shifts when the self is struggling with other life issues. When we take the time to support the self in this manner, it feels safer and thus will more readily return to the task at hand: learning.

Teacher Illustration 3.5: Managing a Group Resistance

Amy Smith, English Teacher, Ramapo High School, Franklin Lakes, NJ

The tenth-grade class was discussing King Arthur's decision making in T. H. White's *The Once and Future King.* To personalize the difficulty of making decisions, I asked the class what important decisions they had ever made and what they had to take into consideration to make those decisions. As this was a very affluent district, the decisions generally included where to go on vacations or what type of watch they should buy.

Alexis, however, was new to the district but didn't share the affluence of the others. She was living in a group home and was just trying to assimilate to her very new and unusual environment. She exuded a tough exterior, developed over the years she spent in foster care and group homes, and she tended not to say much in class. After the third student told the class of the difficulty of deciding which car her parents were going to buy her for her birthday, Alexis had had enough. She knocked her chair over as she shot up from her desk, and as she stormed to the door, she screamed, "You can all go to hell!" As she reached the door, I called her name, as I was trying to assuage her anger. She turned on me as she slammed the door and screamed, "F*CK YOU!" After the door slammed, there was silence in the room, yet some students were unsure about their reaction and started to look at each other and giggle. There was no going back to the discussion of the book. The group dynamic had to be addressed.

I asked the class for their opinions about why Alexis had reacted the way she did. Since not many of the students knew her background, but only saw her tough exterior, they only guessed that she was jealous. For the next 15 minutes, we discussed what possible situations may have initiated Alexis's behavior. I then was able to relate the conversation to decision making, as they all had to decide how they were going to handle their next encounter with Alexis as well as their classroom discussions from that point on. The discussion made them realize that decisions in life not only concerned themselves, but often, concerned the welfare of others: exactly what King Arthur had to do.

Intervention 3.6: Intent Versus Content

Spotting a defense, labeling it, and choosing an intervention can feel like a daunting task. So if you initially feel overwhelmed and in the midst of a chaotic classroom, here is a general rule of thumb: Listen for the *intent* of a comment or disruption, rather than the *content* and intervene accordingly. What may be bothering your student? What need is calling out to be met? What does the disruption achieve for the student?

When you find yourself exasperated by a student's disruptive behavior, try thinking to yourself, *How is this action or behavior protecting the student? What is the motivation behind the words?* The content may be "You are the worst teacher ever," but the intent is probably, *I am scared. I might fail.* The former takes the responsibility of failure from the self and displaces it onto the teacher. (The ego hates the hot seat and would rather displace or project—both of which are defenses—negativity onto you or someone or something else.) Our task then would be to make his or her self feel safe and empowered (rather than to defend our teaching): "My teaching may be a problem, yes . . ." (disarming and gaining attention) ". . . but it sounds as though you are really frustrated with the material as well (mirroring). This material is quite challenging . . ." (validation, object oriented). "Let me see if I can teach in a way that better meets your needs." (Take the ego off the hot seat.) Yes! This may sound a bit awkward on paper, but when delivered in a friendly tone and a smile (delivery is important!), the student is likely to feel more connected to you, less stressed and more open to learning. And, incorporating all of those interventions in a few sentences will become more and more natural. Remember, if your students are defended and stressed, cognition will shut down faster than the classroom clears at the bell. *Learning opens up, when defenses come down.* Supporting the self helps to soften the defenses.

Example 3.6: Looking at Intent—
Cheating on the Sports Field

When kids cheat during sports, the underlying feeling is likely incompetence or fear of failure. This is what we mean by focusing on intent rather than content. The content, "I swear he never tagged me," is a lie, but the intent is to save the self from failure. Yes, it's a defense, but looking at the intentions will help you find the reason lurking behind it.

When we recognize that a child is afraid of failing or losing, we can then select interventions that lessen the fear and support the self. In this case, instead of insisting that he was tagged and that you saw it, you might use mirroring and simply say, "Losing can be tough sometimes can't it?" When he continues to insist he didn't lose, you could explore something like, "What would it mean to you if you had?" or "Okay, you weren't tagged. Tagging may feel terrible, but playing well and fairly feels great." The subconscious will hear the intention behind your comments as well.

Try to help a student see that enjoying the game, the process, is what matters. Did he play well? Make a big effort? Learn anything? Have fun? In today's world, sometimes students have been taught that winning is the endgame rather than having fun or putting in a large effort. We suggest supporting the self that wants to have fun.

CHAPTER SUMMARY

Check In With Your Self

On a scale from easy to impossible, how do you rate your ability to accept your students for who they are? _____

| 1 (easy) | 5 (tough, but manageable) | 10 (impossible) |

How do you rate your ability to connect with your students, each one of them?

_____

What have you done recently to let your most "difficult" students know that despite your differences, you accept them and value them?

Interventions

Object-oriented language

Validation

Scaffolding

Mirroring

Managing a group resistance

Look at intent over content

Activity: Soften Defenses

Situation	Goal	Intervention
Describe a situation you hope to improve.	What do you hope to achieve with the student?	Which intervention in the chapter will you use?
Lea is extremely shy and does not seem to have much confidence in her writing skills.	*Showing the student her potential and giving her the confidence to share it with me, and possibly the class.*	*Scaffolding* *Mirror her potential, not her insecure feelings*

Outcome
List the time frame and overall impressions.
For 3 weeks, I thought Lea might fail my class. Then I stopped trying to reach her in front of everyone and spoke to her privately, encouraging her. On the last assignment, I showed her how each element she had written was strong and allowed her to rewrite parts that did not contribute to the overall quality. She appears more relaxed in class. Her first draft of the latest essay is particularly detailed and strong.

Now construct a chart from your experience.

The Aware Emotional Self: Provide Tools for Emotional Management

Emotionally supportive classrooms *[emphasis added] are related to greater student motivation, interest, enjoyment and engagement, better student coping strategies, less violent behavior, and greater school adjustment and academic achievement.*

—As quoted in Brackett, Reyes, Rivers, Elbertson, & Salovey (2011, p. 27)

WHAT YOU WILL LEARN IN THIS CHAPTER

This chapter introduces Step 3: Provide tools for emotional management. After reading this chapter, you will know

- Steps to emotional awareness
- The process toward emotional management
- Techniques to foster students' emotional awareness and management
- More about the emotional self in the classroom
- Strategies and interventions to be emotionally supportive when classroom frustrations arise

EMOTIONAL AWARENESS: KNOWING YOUR TEMPERATURE

How can you teach teens to think before they text? To think and consider the consequences before accepting a drink? To breathe deeply, pause, and think before lashing out in your classroom? To manage emotions when in the hallways so that they are present in the science lab? You begin by developing emotional awareness and supporting emotional management with your words, lessons, and actions. Because once emotions overwhelm your students, learning shuts down. Until the mind and the psyche are aware of and able to manage emotions, the students will be distracted by thoughts and feelings that will inhibit the cognitive self from a free-flowing openness to learning.

Chapter 2 focused on how to manage thoughts and emotions outside a student's awareness: This chapter focuses on recognizing and managing more *conscious emotions.*

Realizing, Labeling, and Sourcing Emotions

Emotional awareness includes the following steps:

Realizing that an emotion is occurring

Labeling that emotion

Recognizing the source of that emotion

1. *Realizing* that an emotion is holding you hostage from being the best that you can be in any given situation is the first step necessary to achieving emotional awareness— emotions are energy, that's why you feel them! Imagine this: You are standing in a room, and suddenly, the hairs on your arms start to stand up and you shiver. You feel cold. This causes you to think, *It's getting cold in here.* This prompts you to look around for the source of the feeling. You notice the window is wide open. You shut it. Quite simple, eh?

But without awareness of feeling cold and the thought, *Hey it's getting cold in here,* you would have been pretty unlikely to look around for the

> **Check In With Your Self**
>
> What is the most recent intense negative emotion you've experienced? Were you aware of it in the moment? Did you acknowledge and recognize the source of the emotion? Does realizing the source of the emotion help you manage subsequent scenarios that may trigger the emotion? Then what did you do? Were you happy with the result? If you were unaware of the source at the time, are you aware now? Remember this emotion. You will refer to it again shortly.

source: the open window. Likewise, if you feel tension mounting and your heart pumping and you think to yourself, *Hey I am getting angry,* then you are more likely to look around and find the source of your anger (a friend, a parent, an injustice, who knows?). *Emotional awareness makes possible the action of finding a solution and effecting emotional management.* But the first step to emotional awareness is checking in with your feelings and recognizing they are occurring. Being emotionally *unaware* precludes proactive strategies going forward.

2.   Once you realize that an emotion is occurring, the next step is to *label* the emotion. The language of emotions can often be difficult for some students (and adults). Our society often discourages us from talking openly about emotions, and this subsequently inhibits our ability to properly label them. For instance, when you were young, you might have learned that the buzzing flying thing in your room was a fly. The next time you saw a buzzing flying thing in your room, you shouted "Fly!" but your parents smiled and corrected you and said, "No, that's a mosquito," or "No, that's a bee." Not all buzzing flying things are the same, and neither are your buzzing, flying emotions. Being able to distinguish between their subtle differences not only helps you to locate the source, but also to take the appropriate action (squash it, enjoy it, help remove it . . . you choose . . .). Accurately labeling emotions is a skill, and like any other, the more it is practiced and refined, the greater the potential for its use. When emotions are difficult or uncomfortable to accurately identify and label, defenses may develop (displacement, denial, projection are all examples of this).

3.   Labeling the emotion is equally important as the next step: *Locating the source* of an emotion. Sometimes this is as simple as finding an open window. For example, you are working on your quantum physics dissertation and suddenly realize that you feel quite irritated. When you stop to wonder why, you realize that your teen's techno music is blaring in the next room. You, of course, kindly go and ask your lovely obliging teen to turn down the music and, voila! Your head begins to clear. However, finding a source is not always that easy. Teens often find themselves raging at their parents when the real source of their anger is a friend who hurt them earlier in the day (defense = displacement). Or a teen might feel lonely and simply be unsure why she feels so lonely when her three best friends are all giggling beside her. Sources are not always easy to find. Being able to find the proper source of an emotion is a skill that develops with practice.

Consider This

Beware of the blame game when locating sources. Finding the cause of emotions is an important part of awareness and, ultimately, management. It will help you and your students determine coping strategies and effective courses of action. However, teens need to take responsibility for their emotions. Emotions are often the result of a subjective interpretation of an experience. As such, nothing is *inherently* annoying, irritating, sad, or ridiculous. A teen may find his little brother completely annoying while his friend finds the little brother hilarious. The brother isn't inherently annoying (or hilarious). But the teen experiences his little brother that way and the responsibility of managing his emotional reaction falls to the teen and not to the little brother.

Fostering Emotional Awareness: Using the Steps Above in the Classroom

In order to bring forth more emotional awareness in your students, focus on developing the three separate components just reviewed: awareness, labeling, and sourcing. To do this, begin by making emotions a common language in your classroom, regardless of what grade you teach:

- Label and talk about emotions when they occur in the classroom or in context to a topic. The more you talk about emotions, the more you provide a common language and acceptance for them in the lives of your students.
- Try to become specific with those emotions by using different words for them. Anxiety can be accompanied by agitation, nervousness, fear, and/or confusion. Which are your students feeling?
- Develop emotional vocabulary: Have them use several words to describe their emotional state. Have them note which ones they are not.
- Validate group emotions publicly and individual emotions privately—when appropriate.
- Mirror the unaware emotions present in a discussion, incident, etc.
- Recognize and share positive emotions, not just negative ones. Noting the positive feelings in a room helps to build and spread them, while also allowing students to fully experience them. (Sometimes positive emotions are neglected in an effort to return to the task at hand.)

Teacher Illustration 4.1: Emotional Awareness

Kristin Hiemstra, School Counselor, Chapel Hill, NC

Mara was a sophomore when I noticed real changes in her: Once quiet but serious and engaged, she began to retreat and ask to go to the bathroom frequently. Her grades slipped, and she demonstrated less control over her urges (using her cell phone during class). One day, she arrived with her hair dyed bright green. Then, her Tumblr account was brought to my attention. Her page displayed horrific images of teen girls cutting themselves and a love letter to Anna (Anna being the code name for anorexia). Appropriate interventions were made (professionals brought in, parents alerted) in an effort to help and support Mara. She had not made the correlation between what she chose to focus her attention on and how she felt about herself and her academics. Mara realized she needed to change peer groups, as her social life was the catalyst to her troubles. The dark and lonely vibe she gave off only attracted the same type of people into her life. We discussed the fact that both positives and negatives were happening all the time and that she had a choice about what to focus her attention on. She took down her Tumblr page after realizing that every time she looked at it, she felt worse about herself. As she became aware of where her attention flowed, she began to make changes in her behaviors. She looked for things going well and began acknowledging that good things were happening in her life. By taking little steps and monitoring her own thinking, she made huge strides in defeating the negative nellies.

Below are more concrete examples to immediately begin helping students with the process of recognizing, labeling, and sourcing emotions:

1. Use Local or International News to Spur Discussions on Emotions

Expand timely discussions to include the emotional content. For example, if the star kicker on the football team missed the winning field goal, discuss how he might be feeling today (but not if he is in the classroom and definitely without shaming the person). Or, choose a trendy celebrity known to your age group who has had a setback— what might he or she be feeling in the midst of the paparazzi? Extrapolate to other people involved: What might his manager be feeling? His mom? His rival? If you teach history, ask about the feelings a historical character may have had. If you teach science, ask what Thomas Edison may have felt when he tried his 100th light bulb and failed. Ask how your students feel during frog dissection. But remember: No feeling is wrong or right. It may be different from the next person's interpretation, but it is not to be judged. Ever.

2. Expand Emotional Vocabulary

After providing a language for emotions, put it to the test by using one of our favorite emotions—humor! Check in with your students and see how creative, descriptive, and accurate they can be each day as you ask how they are. You will not only prompt students to recognize their emotions, but when done well, promote connections. Who can find the most interesting word to describe his or her emotion that day? Bonus points may be given for use of that word in upcoming essays and reports.

3. Practice "Sourcing" Emotions

Emotions that are not properly sourced or managed can become defenses and may spill over into different situations (projection, displacement, repression)—a key reason why emotional awareness and management are so important. To help illustrate this, relate how a parent can have a bad day at work, come home and slam the door, or yell at a child. The parent clearly hasn't dealt with whatever happened at work to incite his or her anger so he or she displaces it at home. Ask if your students can relate. Can they share stories of times when they were angry with someone, but the real source of their emotion was something else? Have they ever "slammed a door" so to speak?

To help practice finding sources, have students offer multiple sources for different emotional situations. For instance, if you are discussing world politics and a particular politician appears to be angry, ask students to offer their ideas (especially less conventional ideas) on why that person could be angry: "He can't get world leaders to see his point of view" is one reason, but so are "His wife is angry with him because he is spending too much time at work," "His political friends have abandoned him," and even, "He has heartburn." Have your students constantly offer multiple sources of emotion for common situations. This will increase their own ability to find all the sources that are contributing to their emotions when necessary and to have empathy for people who are just having a bad day.

EMOTIONAL MANAGEMENT: SHUTTING THE WINDOW

Emotional management is vital to learning, decision making, and healthy interpersonal relationships. Without skills to manage emotions, emotions become overwhelming and shut down the neurological pathways in the brain that promote learning, impulse control, and memory. When that happens, even the most incredibly entertaining and experienced teacher will not be able to get a simple text into his students' brains. (Chapter 5 goes into greater detail on this.)

Students may arrive to your classroom with little to no emotional management skills. In fact, their skill sets may consist of maladaptive management techniques: They impulsively and sometimes destructively react to situations instead of responding with well-thought-out decisions.

> **Check In With Your Self**
>
> Self-awareness comes in handy for teachers because days can be stressful, emotional, and demanding. What are you doing to become aware of your emotions, manage them, and deal with them constructively, all while helping students with their own issues? Knowing how to manage your self will help your students do the same.
>
> Are you "walking the walk" or just "talking the talk"?
>
> How do your students view you?
>
> When you are tired and stressed, do you hide it? Show it? Share it? What feels right to you? What are your boundaries?

The Process

Bob trips Jake—Jake punches Bob.

Emotional management allows for the space and time for awareness to have an effect on the subsequent response. With emotional management skills, the process looks more like this:

Bob trips Jake—Jake checks in with his emotions, *I feel angry with Bob.* Then Jake thinks, *What is up with that? What should I do?*—Jake says, "Hey dude, what's up? You just totally tripped me." Now they have a dialogue rather than a brawl.

Check In With Your Self

Remember that recent emotion on which we asked you to reflect earlier? If you could change the initial reaction you had as a result of that emotion, would you? If so, how does pausing to consider your thoughts and feelings (or perhaps even the previously unrealized source of the emotion) contribute to a new response? Does the process help you become more in touch with your self?

Responding to emotionally charged incidents in a way that resonates with who you choose to be is emotional management. As you move students through exercises to increase their awareness, they become better equipped to manage their responses. Self education (teaching to the self), and indeed, social emotional learning (SEL) programs in general, help students gain control over their responses. Their responses are ultimately an expression of their self; choosing how to respond rather than react makes life easier for them.

Few things are more empowering for a student than to realize she has control over the way she responds to both her emotions and the situation. So little of a student's life is in his control (in his eyes). Telling and showing students that they do have control, that they can handle difficult situations, is a powerful way to motivate them and solidify their self. Incidentally, teaching them that taking responsibility (and thereby control) rather than blaming others (loss of control) keeps them in the driver's seat of their interactions.

The following diagram shows that thought and emotion patterns can become cyclical, particularly because the cycle works in the other direction as well: Emotions can influence our thoughts, which may influence our experiences. As such, managing thoughts and emotions can be a powerful deterrent to negative moods that seem to spiral out of control.

Try filling in the diagram with the thoughts and feelings from the reflections you've made while thinking about a recent emotional experience and your thoughts about it.

The cyclical nature of our thoughts, emotions, and experiences.

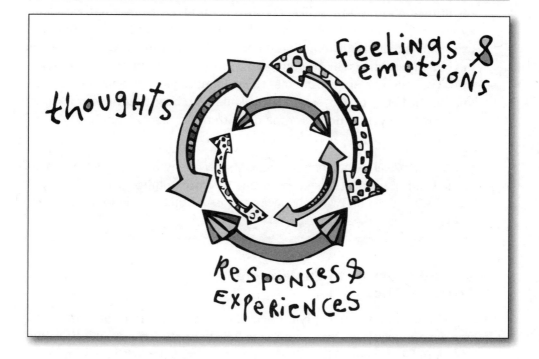

When students understand the power of their thoughts—and that they can alter them—they can begin to manage their emotions. Below are two ways to explain this to your students.

First Example to Explain the Power of Thoughts

Provide your students with the following example: you have an experience—Sam asks you out on a date—you think, *OMG!!! Help! Is he joking? Serious? What do I do?* With thoughts such as those, let your students see that they are likely to then feel *nervous, confused, and scared.* What happens then? They are likely to respond in a way that is apprehensive and timid, "Um, well, I, uh, . . ." which causes them to think, *OMG, I sound like such an idiot!!!* They then feel even more nervous and continue the downward spiral.

Like a watchdog for unwanted intruders, monitoring our thoughts protects against negative feelings and subsequent responses. In the date example, imagine if the thought became, *Hmmm, I'm not sure what I want to do.* This thought, although still unsure, mitigates the nervousness and takes the pressure off the self. Students realize that with this thought, they are less likely to get as nervous, so their subsequent emotions tend to be more subdued, turning into something like *unsure and even a bit excited.* They can see that their response will be influenced by their thoughts and resulting emotions—most likely positively (or at least closer to their ideal) such as, "I'm not sure if I can go. I'll let you know." The first reaction example (the dramatic, emotional one) is likely to hinder academic focus in your classroom as the student may continue to ruminate over her reaction. The second response enables the student to place the emotional content on the back burner—at least until after you have taught your lessons.

Now have your students come up with their own examples.

> Our example is a common social situation for a reason. We suggest beginning with a simple, common issue, one to which both genders can easily relate. Then you may wish to move on to issues that pertain to the disturbances in your classroom.

Second Example to Explain the Power of Thoughts

The second way to explain the cyclical nature of thoughts, emotions, and experiences is with an exercise to help your students create their own emotional awareness. Have your students spend a day with pads and pencils for them to jot down every time they have a negative thought about their *self.* Once gathered, have the class volunteer some of the themes of their thoughts (handed in privately, if necessary). No doubt, you will see how sorely needed emotional management is—teens' thoughts tend to be very self-critical. As an intervention, suggest that for a day, they catch themselves each time they have a negative thought (*I am so ugly, my thighs are fat, I stink at basketball*). Each negative thought must be replaced with a positive thought, which students can brainstorm together in class (*I am fabulous, my legs get me where I need to go, basketball may not be my best sport, but dance is*). Follow up to discuss the two different experiences.

This lesson has several benefits: First, it highlights that many students are experiencing similar thought patterns, providing them with a common bond and normalizing their experience (this validates and builds the self). Second, it starts to teach them that there is a different way—that they do have control over what goes on in their minds. You are planting the seed that they can change the way they view themselves and the world, that emotional management can become a lifetime habit. By changing the way they think about things and about themselves, they can change the way they *experience* life.

Teacher Illustration 4.2: The Power of a Thought Journal

Chris Parrott while working at the Mawbey Brough Centre, London, England

While working with young teens, I would often employ this exercise. Teens are practically preprogrammed with negative self-talk. The fact that their self-talk was completely outside of their awareness, and often contributing to and maintaining their depression, was lost on them. Keeping a thought journal was an absolute eye-opener for them. Quite often, they would enter my office with sheepish looks on their faces and say, "Oh crap—I really am my own worst enemy!" For those who didn't say this immediately, we would go over their thoughts and test their validity: Were the teens always clumsy? Did truly no one like them? What defines an idiot? I never had a client who did not view the power of his or her thoughts differently after this exercise.

THE EMOTIONAL SELF IN THE CLASSROOM

The rest of this chapter discusses five common classroom disturbances, all of which stem from a lack of emotional awareness and its management. Examples of corresponding interventions to help support the emotional self in its effort to grow are also found.

Classroom Disturbance 1: Bullying

Bullying is an issue of both emotional awareness and emotional management. Most students who bully do so without an awareness of the emotions driving their behaviors. These students have likely been hurt in their lives and are directing that hurt and anger at others (defense mechanism = displacement). Getting to the root of bullying behavior means connecting with the self of the bully and helping him become more aware of his emotions and manage them.

However, the primary emotion we wish bullies to initially recognize is not their anger or hurt, but their capacity for empathy. Here's why: Very few differences exist between a bully and a leader (or a popular student), save one: empathy, a core component of the self (Haber, 2007). Without the development of empathy, the self can feel disconnected from others, making ripe a disposition primed for bullying.

Bullying Is a Defense

Bullying behavior is the defense we referred to earlier called acting out. People who bully push others away and avoid connections— *true* connections. Most likely they have been hurt in the past and see hurting others as both a way to release their anger and protect themselves: *Get away from me, otherwise you might hurt me. Let me see how much I can project my hurt onto you and see you in the pain that I feel but won't acknowledge.* Heavy. We know. But social skills, empathy, and making those connections will go so much farther in helping an atmosphere plagued by bullying than will any lecture on the statistics, causes, and consequences.

Empathy is what allows us to relate to and understand another's feelings. It is what connects one self to another. We have what are called *mirror neurons* located in the dorsolateral prefrontal cortex, that actually "mirror" the emotions of others, thereby connecting our emotions with others, proof that we are wired for empathy (Horstman, 2009). This wiring is what allows a student to understand another's frustration (including yours) and to possibly adjust his or her behavior accordingly. It allows the person who bullies to recognize the pain she is causing and, therefore, change her patterns of bullying. Becoming *aware* of one's feelings of empathy allows the person who is bullying to *manage* her behavior. This is the first line of defense against bullying. Long-term change occurs when empathy is continually fostered and the self (through the interventions in these chapters) becomes strong and whole.

Intervention 4.1: Promote Empathy

Below are some strategies to help you foster empathy, an innate capacity in all of us that flourishes when both practiced and experienced.

a. Use characters in a book (an object-oriented exercise!).

Have students discuss how they relate to or feel about characters in stories. When a character is a victim, have every child talk about what that means and how they feel about watching the "victim." What emotions do they experience reading the material? (See Chapter 3 "Example 3.1: Using Object-Oriented Examples and Language.")

b.   Turn the tables.

Continually ask the question, "How would you feel if . . . *(fill in the blank with whatever a person did to another)* happened to you?" The person who bullied has a wounded self in need of repair. The first step in the repair is for her to recognize *(become aware of)* the feelings that she has created in another. When a bully can connect her own (self) feelings to those of another, she can also begin to understand the implications and be motivated to change. Another way to achieve a similar outcome is to use historical or famous figures: "How did the poor, sick, and orphaned in India feel when Mother Theresa showed up?"

Example 4.1: Famous People and Their Character

Morality and character provide a foundation for healthy self-conduct, another antidote to bullying. Therefore, discussions about these deep core issues of the self will help students begin to self-reflect and gain emotional awareness. To do so, create a writing assignment based on one or more of the following:

Was Genghis Khan a bully? Who would say yes? Who would say no? Describe "character." Describe the character of two or more of the following: Julius Caesar, Hitler, Mother Theresa, Oprah Winfrey, Simon Cowell, Donald Trump, Joe Paterno, etc. What are some differences between them (and you)? Similarities? How do their actions affect others or society at large? What are some of the emotions people felt as a result of the actions of this person?

If you were a close friend of this person, what would you have done: supported their actions, stood against them, or done nothing? Why? How do your actions—as the pretend friend to this person—represent your moral code and affect the people around you? How might your actions affect your school or community? How do you relate your thoughts about this person to what's happening in your life now?

The last few questions are important because they bring the discussion back to the self.

Intervention 4.2: Know the Language of Bullying in Your School

Bullying—both overt and covert—reaches far and wide. Not one lesson plan or preventative program exists to extinguish the tentacles of this monstrous epidemic. What does exist, and what does effect change, is a continuous system of addressing the debris clogging the container: filling the voids in character development and validating the essence of your students. These crucial steps begin with a common language, and that language is likely neither yours, nor ours, but theirs.

Psychological aggression, drama, and relationship conflict are all ways to explain the many different forms that bullying takes, on and off campus. But students' translations include words such as "drama," "relationship issues," or even "whatever, like, you know, stuff happens." Knowing their language helps to reach and impact the self. Too many antibullying programs fail to do this, and students miss the connection between what they are experiencing and what the presentation is saying. Using adult and media language does not necessarily connect with them. Using their language will. Listen in your hallways, before class starts, on the sports field, and even in the words of their essays for verbiage that will connect with their experiences.

Example 4.2: The Language of Bullying

Shaniqua is in ninth grade. She says to her "friend" Rachel, "Yo, what were you thinking when you threw that freakish outfit together? Just kidding! *(Pause)* Oh shut up, you're not, like, getting all emotional on me, are ya? Can't you take a joke?"

This type of talk could be okay if Rachel and Shaniqua are the closest of friends, and it is clear between the two of them that they are "playing." However, if any power differential or relationship insecurities exist, this type of talk is termed relational bullying. It puts Rachel in a near impossible situation to respond while Shaniqua is most likely unaware of the hurt her words can cause. If she is aware of it, she needs to learn a bit more compassion. To bring forth an awareness of relational bullying, have your class think of phrases that are common language but that actually hurt the recipient. Just bringing forth this awareness may shift the dialogue. Taken one step further, brainstorm secret codes students may use to remind each other to be conscious of their use of language and to choose their words more carefully. Identifying language that is subtly hurtful helps students to be more aware of the emotional impact they have on each other. Without constant verbal attacks, the self is strengthened.

Intervention 4.3: Use Praise Over Punishment

Remember the story about the sun and the wind in competition for which could make the man on the park bench remove his overcoat faster? The wind blew as furiously as he could, but the man only clutched his coat closer to himself in protection. Then the sun had a stab at it and shone down on the man, who promptly felt the warmth and removed his outer layer.

The analogy is easy to see: A teacher who beats down punitively on a student will get nowhere as the student clutches closer to his or her protective armor. But the teacher who lets the support and connection grow will have a far greater effect—enabling the student to open up and feel more comfortable.

Praise (of effort, in particular) has a longer psychic shelf life than punishment, which only reinforces to the student that he or she is bad in the first place.

And sometimes when students feel they can't do anything right, they begin to project those feelings to the outside world—to act out in ways that are maladaptive.

Classroom Disturbance 2: Acting Out and Impulse Control

Dr. Walter Mischel is known for his famous "marshmallow" study of the 1960s. He and his colleagues studied self-control among young children. In a room with the researcher, individual children were told they had a choice to eat a marshmallow (or similar treat) immediately, or if they could just wait until the researcher returned, they could eat two. Those who *were not able to wait* to eat the marshmallow were later found to have more behavioral issues in school and at home, got lower SAT scores, had poorer coping strategies, had trouble paying attention, had a higher Body Mass Index, and were found to have difficulty maintaining friendships and careers. The children who could wait 15 minutes or longer had an SAT score that was, on average, 210 points higher than that of the child who could not wait (Tough, 2012).

This study has led to a firestorm of activity in the psycho-educational community. If intelligence is no longer an accurate predictor of academic performance, but self-control is, then how can we apply these findings in the classroom? Walter Mischel describes the more patient children: "This task forces kids to find a way to make the situation work for them. They want the second marshmallow, but how can they get it? We can't control the world, but we can control how we think about it." The students who waited for the second marshmallow did so by distracting themselves with counting, singing a song, or pacing around the room. Mischel says, "Once you realize that will power is just a matter of learning how to control your attention and thoughts, you can really begin to increase it" (Lehrer, 2009).

Lest we forget, this idea of using the mind to control our thoughts and subsequent behavior is what we have been discussing in this very chapter. But, self-control is an emotional management skill. Children wanted the marshmallow, but some were able to manage that want and some were not. Like any skill, it comes more naturally to some, but it can be developed by most. Students today benefit from learning the dynamics involved in self-control and the techniques needed to strengthen theirs. In the area of self-control, emotional awareness and thought monitoring techniques are quite helpful as is a student's understanding that his or her attention to, or distraction from, an issue can be the difference needed to reach his or her goals. By using such techniques, students are more apt to find their way from point A to point B without being distracted by a party, exclusion, a fashion trend, snacks, monetary issues, and the like.

Intervention 4.4: Develop a Plan; Define the Endgame

In your classroom, help students recognize what their goals are—define the endgame in your lesson for the week, or the semester. For instance, let's say you'll be administering the state exams in 2 weeks. Have your students write an essay or make a chart (not to be graded) on what they aim to achieve, how they will reach their goals and, most important, what they will do when they become distracted. This last element is critical: Many students do not have strategies to mediate their emotions when the going gets tough. They are the students who did not know to sing a song to distract themselves from the marshmallow, and now they will need help determining how to distract themselves from the elements (Facebook, iChat, texting, sports games, etc.) that may hinder them from reaching their goals. Have them return to their essays or charts to refocus themselves on their goals and to help replace negative thoughts with more positive ones.

Validating struggles and encouraging students in their efforts are key to building self-control. In times of difficulty, ask them to reflect on their original goals and objectives. This process helps them become closer to the self to which they aspire, builds character, and recognizes their personal impediments to feeling successful. When students self-reflect on the process necessary to reach an end goal, their personal distractions become less powerful. Students not hard-wired for this process need your encouragement and scaffolding until they are comfortable with the idea of making a plan and figuring out how to stick to it.

Classroom Disturbance 3: Aggressive Behavior

Comfort in expressing your emotions will allow you to share the best of yourself with others, but not being able to control your emotions will reveal your worst.

—Bryant H. McGill

Aggressive behavior can be adaptive or maladaptive. When teens sublimate their aggression into sports or drama, they are finding adaptive ways to release the stress or frustration associated with the aggressive impulse. But when aggression is demonstrated in hurtful ways, then adults often need to intervene. Simply put, *the emotion underlying the aggressive act needs reflection, awareness, adaptive release, and further management.*

Of course, this is not in your job description, but like many other issues in the classroom, unless you address this issue, learning will not take place. When the brain is stressed, the student goes into "fight, flight, or freeze" mode. The fight mode brings forth the aggressive behavior, limiting learning both for the aggressor and for your entire class. Awareness of what causes that stress, and techniques to manage it are actually within your reach as a teacher, although we recognize that aggression management is no easy task.

Intervention 4.5: Seek to Find Success

To calm aggressive behavior and help the student become more in touch with the emotion driving behavior, privately walk her through a series of questions. If you find the driving emotion exceptionally worrisome *(I feel homicidal. I feel suicidal. I want to torture small animals. I look for ways to hurt people online, etc.)*, please refer the student to the school counselor, being especially careful of confidentiality issues, and follow up to make sure the student is receiving support. The steps below reflect *the questions* you will be asking the student (again, privately):

1. Ask, "What feeling motivated your behavior just now?" Make sure the answer is a feeling/emotion and not a thought (i.e., "I was angry" versus "I thought John was being mean").

2. Ask, "Why were you *(the emotion)*?" Help them make a connection between the origin of the feeling and the source. Is the source direct or could multiple sources be at work? (The anger will be the conscious emotion, but an unconscious source is likely to be adding to that feeling). *I was angry that John cut me in line.*

3. Ask, "How does (*name the destructive/aggressive behavior*) help you handle the situation? Who is hurt as a result?" The point here is to help the student identify with the negative repercussions of her choice of actions. *I hit him to teach him a lesson that you don't cut in line, but I ended up getting in trouble, and now everyone is looking at me.* Incidentally, this is a good time to use some empathy training, such as, "How would you feel if someone hit you for cutting in line?"

4. Ask, "What are some other ways you could deal with this emotion in the future?" Emotions are bound to resurface, so brainstorm some strategies so that the student feels more in control of her emotions. Those strategies may be as simple as telling an adult about the situation or walking away. Let the student find strategies that feel right for her. Try moving toward more adaptive defenses. Use humor, sublimation, or rationalization to illustrate new ways to manage emotions. "Cutting in line is wrong. I agree with you. But hitting is wrong. How else can you deal with it?" Empathy: "How would you like someone to handle it if you cut in line?"

Recognize and praise progress. Students are motivated to do something only when they feel they are capable of meeting the challenge in front of them. If a child has a long history of aggressive behavior, she may not feel capable of coming to a complete stop right away. This is why small steps are important. Even screaming may be better for some students than hitting if they are so prone to violence. Work with students to find something they feel capable of trying and then recognize any efforts made toward that.

Intervention 4.6: Index Cards for Temper Management

If you have a student who is having a difficult time controlling his or her temper, have him or her construct an index card for personal self-reflection and habit-changing behavior. I (Parrott) found great success while working in London using this approach. Construct the card as follows:

Right now I am feeling: _____

At times I have lost control of my temper when I have felt_____.
When I feel this way, I used to _____.
Now when I begin to feel _____, I have chosen the follow-
ing strategies to help me make better choices and deal proactively with my
temper:

1.   2.   3.

This brings awareness and responsible action, rather than repetitive maladaptive behavior to the mind and the self. Also, notice that it places the negative behavior in the past and affirms the new self in the present and going forward.

Teacher Illustration 4.6: Index Cards for Temper Management

Chris Parrott while working at the Mawbey Brough Centre, London, England

Franco was a young teen being raised in a very abusive household when I met him. His stepfather was an alcoholic and often flew into rages. As Franco hit puberty, he found he often flew into rages himself. We were able to determine that his anger stemmed from feeling both unappreciated and powerless. A sample card for Franco read, "Right now, I am feeling attacked, angry, and powerless. In the past when I felt this way, I would attack back. Now when I begin to feel angry and powerless, I have chosen the following strategies to help me make better choices and deal with my temper. 1. I remind myself that I have the power to be who I want to be. 2. I can leave. 3. I can take a deep breath and say, 'I feel angry right now. I feel like you are attacking me.'" Franco reported positive changes through using this method: "Those cards remind me of who I have chosen to be, not what my anger chooses to be. I can think better in the moment rather than rage."

Classroom Disturbance 4: Spacing Out

As noted with aggression, overwhelming emotions cause the flight, fright, or freeze reactions in your students. Aggression is the manifestation of fight mode. Spacing out is "freezing" (Willis, 2011a). It happens when an experience has provoked a student to become distant, perhaps as an escape mechanism. She then habitually drifts off to other planets, rarely touching down on earth. Seeing students space out in your classroom can be quite frustrating to you, as you know they are not absorbing the information. It can also be quite frustrating to other students when, as the result of spacing out, some students cannot keep up with the class. Cries to "Pay Attention!" work only for seconds before that blank stare returns. When provided with tools for emotional awareness and management, less freezing takes place.

Intervention 4.7: For the Space Traveler—Tap the Desk

Privately, offer to create a secret signal with students who take mini-vacations during class. For example, a gentle tap on his desk when you see Carlos entering never-never land helps refocus his attention, feel supported by your efforts, and the subtle signal saves him from embarrassment.

Though this intervention provides an effective Band-Aid for your intermittent astronaut, your student is also best served by interventions that deal with the root of the spacing out problem.

The root of the spacing out could have a neurological cause (which would need to be addressed) or it could be an emotional/social one. In the latter case, a spaced out student may need stronger connections and some container work in order to bring her back down to earth. When repairs are made to the container through appropriate interventions, your knuckles will no longer need Band-Aids from countless knockings because you will have been proactive in thwarting future space missions.

- Find ways to connect with this student (the tapping is a good start—it sends the message that you see her, understand her, and are not punishing her).
- Hear what being in your class feels like to her, as her feelings may often have been ignored and thus, she spaces out instead of dealing with them.
- Try to polish her core container. For instance, when a child hears relentless lectures at home about how naughty she is, how uncoordinated, unruly, or ugly, she may begin to shut out all lectures—including yours (despite how fascinating it is!). A simple reminder that she is supported, safe, and appreciated in class without living up to this false notion of identifying herself as unworthy and incompetent will allow her to find new self-concepts and definitions. (*Listening has benefits. I don't have to be what others have told me I am. Spacing out is a thing of the past.*)
- Sit in a circle: with a dozen or two other eyes on her, she may be less likely to go on vacation.

Teacher Illustration 4.7: Helping a Student to Focus

Amy Smith, English Teacher, Ramapo High School, Franklin Lakes, NJ

When I taught, I never sat at my desk, but walked around the classroom, up and down the aisles. Just keeping such close proximity to the students helped them stay focused. However, if I saw one of my students with that "far away look" or that "dazed" look, I would slowly make my way over to that aisle without bringing attention to the student and gently rest my hand on his or her shoulder and continue to walk. That usually was enough to bring the student back.

Classroom Disturbance 5: General Stress!

Today, students face familial stress, academic pressure, emotional and social concerns, and, well, kids are simply stressed out! When students feel overwhelmed, and underprepared with how to deal with their stress, they are less likely to achieve academic or life potential. As a result, they often turn to risky behaviors to alleviate their stress, and conditions worsen.

Intervention 4.8: Be Clear About Expectations

Simple measures such as monthly calendars of lessons and homework, review packets, time charts, access to you, test dates, and extra help sessions all help students to better manage their stress. Continually support them in their *effort* to succeed. "Yesterday, Franco made an excellent observation about erosion in South America. Who can remember what that was?" Franco may be far from your best student, but when you give value to students' contributions versus their achievements (i.e., posting test scores), the self feels supported, the container reinforced (Dweck, 2006). As the self is supported, stress is alleviated.

More information on combating stress in your classroom and throughout your school is found in Chapter 5: "The Cognitive Self."

THE BENEFITS

Our cognitive ability to take in information, analyze it, think critically about it, weigh options, and make a decision is an *emotional* as well as cognitive process. But without emotional awareness and management, students fail to make decisions that best reflect who they are. The repercussions are insulting to them and to us. Therefore, very little is more important than supporting the emotional selves of your students. As this chapter illustrates, the self is further developed through emotional awareness and management. When successful, a student is able to

- Label and tolerate feelings
- Deal with conflict
- Cooperate with others
- Come to class on time and be attentive
- Ask and answer questions freely and without self-judgment
- Place more emphasis on work
- Focus, be more attentive
- Smile more

Teaching involves emotional dynamics within the room and within the student-teacher relationship. Below is a YouTube link that poignantly illustrates an environment moving toward emotional awareness, acceptance, and gratitude. The fourth graders are overwhelmed with happiness to discover that they have the same beloved teacher as last year. Watch this video to learn his success, for it is his goal to teach students how to live happy lives and to care for other people (typoprone, 2009): www.youtube .com/watch?v=armP8TfS9Is.

CHAPTER SUMMARY

Check In With Your Self

How do you feel today? Are you aware of your emotions day to day?

Do you ever say to yourself things such as, *She needs to stop making me so angry!* Or, *Raul's attitude is driving me crazy?* With whom is the responsibility placed with such statements? How could you alter those statements to be more in control?

Interventions

Promote empathy

Know the language of bullying in your school

Use praise over punishment

Develop a plan, define the endgame

Seek to find success

Index cards for temper management

Tap the desk

Be clear about expectations

Activity: Foster Emotional Awareness

Situation	Goal	Intervention
Describe a situation you hope to improve. *Mia is constantly late to class and disrespectful.*	What do you hope to achieve with the student? *More respect and better performance.*	Which intervention in the chapter will you use? *Praise*

Outcome
List the time frame and overall impressions.
The first time I praised Mia, she looked at me with evil eyes. I think she thought I was being critical. I think she is used to being reprimanded. After 3 weeks, she is still late most times, but she is considerably less disrespectful.

Now construct a chart from your experience.

The Cognitive Self: Use Cognitive Understanding to Awaken Potentials

One of the key practical lessons of modern neuroscience is that the power to direct our attention has within it the power to shape our brain's firing patterns, as well as the power to shape the architecture of the brain itself.

—Siegel (2010, p. 39)

WHAT YOU WILL LEARN IN THIS CHAPTER

This chapter outlines Step 4: Use cognitive understanding to awaken potentials. In this chapter, you will learn

- Basic brain structure and related functions
- How stress affects the brain
- Interventions for stress
- Neuroplasticity and its implications for learning
- How to improve motivation using the self

Check In With Your Self

From the list below, put a check next to each concept that you could confidently teach to your students tomorrow and explain its importance:

- Hippocampus
- Stress-reduction techniques
- Dopamine
- Executive functions
- Cortisol
- Working memory
- Neuroplasticity
- Amygdala
- Prefrontal cortex

BRAIN STRUCTURE AND RELATED FUNCTIONS

Healthy brain connections depend on healthy human connections.

Self-reflection is the cognitive ability to step outside of oneself and objectively see what one is thinking, feeling, and doing. This important ability can shift the very architecture of your students' brains during a critical time of exponential development. That potential shift stemming from being inwardly mindful includes new social and emotional connections that increase the capacity for resilience, flexibility, empathy, and compassion (Siegel, 2010). Knowing how the mind and brain work facilitates the development of self-reflective capacities, setting the stage for change to take place. Sharing this understanding with your students empowers them to make better decisions, manage stress, and find motivation.

For instance, understanding the mechanics of your bike and how to shift gears appropriately enables you to enjoy your bike ride. You don't get stuck going up hills or pedaling needlessly when speeding downhill. Likewise, understanding brain functions that relate to learning allows you to get the most out of your "learning ride": You can better manage the uphill struggle and optimize the easier territory.

The structures we focus on here include the reticular activating system, the limbic system, the hippocampus, the amygdala, and the prefrontal cortex as they are intrinsically linked to optimal learning because of their unique functions and their locations in the brain (see the illustration below). Once you understand the interplay between these areas, you learn how to put their functions to optimal use.

Imagine your brain as a small town with a few key characters (typical of all small towns) who have unique personalities and roles. Later in the chapter, these areas (townspeople) will be referenced in order for you to put the information provided into practice.

Consider this Phil's brain. Phil is facing left. The regions of the brain discussed below are highlighted.

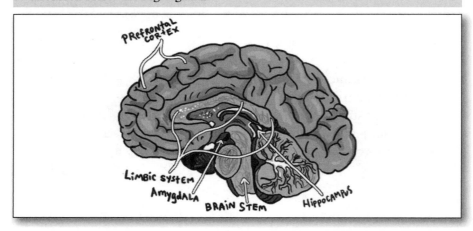

Reticular Activating System (RAS)

Are you presently aware of the billions of bits of information bombarding your senses? You are touching, smelling, listening, seeing, and receiving input from a whole host of stimuli potentially interfering with the integration of this chapter's intriguing information (a crying baby, a noisy neighbor, the bread you put in the oven an hour ago. You're welcome.). But thankfully, a system in your brain called the reticular activating system (RAS) decides what information to attend and what information to disregard (reducing the billions of bits to about 2,000 bits allowed entry) (Willis, 2011a). The RAS is located in the old, reptilian area of our brains, which is encoded for our survival. Therefore, as information enters our RAS, our brain must decide: *Is this necessary for my survival? Is this necessary to help advance my species?* The former requires priority of course, but when we can manage deterrents to the latter, we can improve our state of mind, body, and future of our society.

In our small-town analogy, to be revealed shortly, the RAS is the VIP bouncer who decides who to admit and who to ignore.

Amygdala

After information flows through the RAS, it reaches the limbic system—the emotional center of the brain (shown above). Here, your amygdala and hippocampus (to be discussed below) evaluate just how useful the information from the RAS is and, therefore, what to do with it.

The amygdala is an almond shaped cluster of neuronal activity responsible for deciding where to send the incoming information *based on the emotional state of your students.* When the student is overloaded (stressed or fearful), the amygdala will direct incoming information to the reactive centers of the brain rather than to higher-order processing. Recall, the reactive centers of the brain are responsible for our survival.

During the teen years, the amygdala is primed for stress, anxiety, and fear (in their minds, they are literally trying to survive their day-to-day strife)—all of which inhibit learning. Are your students feeling any of these? If so, they are likely in survival mode, and thus information will not proceed to the higher-level cognitive superhighways of success. Negative emotions—fear, frustration, boredom, sadness—will block information from reaching the higher-order processing area of the brain called the prefrontal cortex. As a result, you will see such things as spacing out, acting out, or even checking out (think survival modes of flight, fright, or freeze), and the wonderful information you are disseminating will not be processed.

To recover, your students will need to shift gears, literally changing their perspective away from survival and toward learning and memory (consolidating learned information). But how? Emotional awareness and management are the first steps (Chapter 4). Focused concentration helps, too. (Like how you brought yourself back from your to-do list when prompted. Thank you for illustrating.)

> Emotion and cognition are linked in the brain. When negative emotions are flying high, cognition is flying low. If you want your students on their cognitive superhighways, help them out of a traffic jam.

Alas, during the teen years especially, the amygdala is our resident "scamp in the 'hood," because it can derail us from the task at hand. (Don't get us wrong, we value the role of the amygdala—it helps keep us safe—but we also recognize the value of knowing how to manage its influence.)

Hippocampus

Memory formation is largely an emotional process, and that is what the hippocampus does: forms memories and connects emotions and senses (the smell of baking bread reminds you of your grandmother) to those memories for later retrieval. Note we are using the word *formation* of new memories. Memories themselves are sent to other areas of the cerebral hemisphere for long-term storage and retrieval (like when you smell bread baking and you instantly remember your grandmother's house and the emotions associated with the experience—that memory was retrieved from a different area of your brain than the hippocampus).

The point here is that emotions, memory, and cognition are linked in the brain. You can see by the diagram that the limbic system (where the amygdala and hippocampus are located) is closely connected to the pre-frontal cortex (discussed below) and to the "old brain" where unconscious bodily functions and survival mechanisms are controlled. This is why the emotional state of your students is very important to monitor. Emotions are linked to all aspects of cerebral function.

And size does matter when it comes to memory formation: The hippocampus increases in size with regular exercise and focused, intense learning. It atrophies as a result of chronic stress, lack of exercise, and chronic inflammation.

> The hippocampus of children raised in loving homes is larger than that of children raised in stressful environments. However, you can have an enormous impact on that growth by following many of the self teaching steps and tips outlined in this book.

Think of the hippocampus like the town historian. He keeps the records and determines what is historically important (memory formation), but if he gets lazy or stressed, his organization skills go out the window.

Prefrontal Cortex (PFC)

As information flows through the limbic system, it may (if not hijacked by the amygdala) be directed to the PFC, the staging area for executive functions. Executive functions include working (or short-term) memory, critical thinking, judgment, creativity, and impulse control. With these abilities students can plan ahead, reason, set goals, problem solve, regulate emotions, and pay attention (wouldn't that be nice in your classroom?). Ultimately, the PFC is where we develop our sense of self, including our moral and empathic skills. Of note, the PFC is *not fully formed* during the teen years. This is why your ability to reach the PFC during the teen years is so vital. It gives you the opportunity to positively impact your students' cognitive abilities *and their self-concepts* that will accompany those abilities.

> Your teens' brains have an amygdala that is primed for stress and fear, coupled with a PFC that is underdeveloped. The implications: Teens are presently wired to be impulsive and to have a hard time accessing the brain centers needed for good decision making—a good thing to consider the next time you find your normally bright student preparing to silly string the principal's office.

The PFC is like a mayor, proactively keeping peace, planning ahead, and organizing events to improve the town. He does so with an even temperament and pleasing personality.

> When you focus on the physical and mental health of your students and teach them ways to control emotions, then more information will flow to the prefrontal cortex.

Putting the Town Together

You likely want your students coming to class with a calm amygdala so that information can have meaning, be processed, and end up in the PFC. However, such an optimal state is not always present. Why not? After all, you are experiencing that state right now while reading this book; unless you begin to think about the garbage to empty, the schedule to make for your kids, the trip you forgot to plan, and the person you need to call. Oops! Your brain just lost focus. But you are smart and resilient. You have a pen and paper to jot down those things so you can do them after you read this chapter. You bring yourself back to task and, voila! Here you are again. Welcome back. (Did you get the bread out of the oven?)

But with teens, the ability to stay on task is not so easily achieved. Imagine their list: Deal with Jose over the fact that Suzy texted Tamara and said Max hates Tomias, which ticked off Sal; bake cookies for mental health awareness fundraiser; figure out why Serge hates me; clean garage before dad yells at me; pick up little sister after school instead of going to the park with friends; oh crud, empty dishwasher; why won't Suzy let me into her science lab?

We can't just have them jot down a list to deal with things later so students can focus now, because their issues are largely more complicated than that; they have not had enough experience to know how to manage them and their PFC is not fully formed. *This chapter suggests interventions so they can manage their concerns and attend to your discussions.* We need to help them use their minds to change their brains, to stay on task, and fire neurons in the direction for academic and life success.

Intervention 5.1: Teach Basic Brain Anatomy and Function

Just how do you manage the emotional status of your students? One way is to teach basic neuroscience to them so that they "get it" and that they can incorporate their cognitive self into their daily functioning. To help present this material to them, use the brain diagram above or download one from the Internet. First, show these key structures and functions. Second, have students label their own diagrams and color them in. Third, tell the following story to your students:

> *You are having a backyard party and you've invited your favorite friends including the town historian, Mr. Hippocampus (so you can remember the party of course!), and the Mayor, Mr. PFC (who also helped you plan the party down to every last detail). You have RAS at the door, deciding who will be allowed to enter as people often crash parties. And guess who crashed this one? Your often infuriating, scamp of a neighbor, Mr. Amygdala. RAS let him through the door! Suddenly you begin to*

notice that your body tenses, that voice in your head begins to freak out, and you lose sight of your wonderful friends and the fun you were just having. You also notice that Mr. PFC is leaving—his potential help fading away faster than the chips and dip. Mr. Hippocampus is literally shrinking in front of your eyes (and here you thought he was only going to get fat from all the hotdogs he inhaled). There goes any chance of even remembering the party!

But then you remember this incredible class you are taking and you become aware of your thoughts and feelings. You see that the situation can only get worse if you continue down this path that Mr. Amygdala has paved for you. If you begin to flip out and yell at him to leave (how dare he show up?!), then your anger will grow—hijacking your ability to enjoy the party.

So instead of allowing Mr. Amygdala to be disruptive, you calmly approach him, invite him over for a beverage, suggest he walk around, and get to know everyone and enjoy the party. Suddenly, Mr. PFC returns and Mr. Hippocampus looks healthy again. Even Mr. Amygdala seems content, which of course has a direct and immediate effect on you, your thoughts, your mood, and your memory.

(Do you know why we suggest presenting this information as a story? Because your students are more likely to remember the brain functions mentioned when the material is given in this format. Your students become the main character, causing involvement, while a storyline creates more meaning, enabling them to better relate to the material. Remember: Cognition, emotion, and memory are linked in the brain.)

As the party analogy illustrates, when the amygdala is calm, the PFC is available for more information, more learning, and more good times. Discuss with your students how the amygdala (which is fully formed in their brains and primed to respond to stressful situations) can "crash their party" and inhibit their PFC abilities, which are still developing. As your students get to know the mechanics of their brains, and how those mechanics impact them, they will have the opportunity to "shift gears" and develop strategies that will keep them from getting stuck or spinning their wheels needlessly. If a student knows she is capable of good decisions, but that she simply may need a little more effort and time for them (see Dr. Baird's work in text box below), her sense of self will be bolstered rather than diminished by a negative perception of her abilities.

Because their PFCs are still maturing, teens' overall thinking, reasoning, and judgment are skewed, as shown by the work of Abigail Baird, associate professor of psychology at Vassar College. Dr. Baird (2010) found that when teens and adults were asked to judge if scenarios were deemed safe or unsafe, the teens' answers were the same as the adults,' but the teens used a different part of their brains to arrive at that same answer. Adults used the amygdala and insula (controls gut reactions—tightening of the viscera) while teens used their PFC to reason through the scenario. Teens were *thinking* through the situation, whereas the adults were *feeling* whether it was safe or not. This is why ample time to think through certain choices is critical: Lack of experience and an underdeveloped PFC translates into the need for more time to think things through.

In Summary

When *something* in your students' life is causing the amygdala to detour information from the PFC, you've lost their cognitive potential. Whether that something is a social, emotional, or psychological issue, your student is effectively in modern day survival mode. Sure, he's not running through the jungle from a dinosaur, but he may be running away from a bully (or his parents' divorce, or his recent romantic rejection).

Ignoring the emotional condition of a student is as dangerous as ignoring a learning disability; cognition is thwarted unless the emotional condition of the child is considered and managed.

How can we calm the amygdala in everyday situations? After all, the less hold that stress, fear, and anxiety have on students' lives, the more potential for learning. Below is a more detailed look at stress and suggestions for interventions so that cognition can flourish.

STRESS ON THE BRAIN

During times of stress, our bodies release the stress hormones cortisol and noradrenaline. An acute shot of these hormones enhances our immune system, boosts activity in the PFC, triggers memory (hippocampus), and provides a burst of energy for cardio needs. You can imagine why this would be a good thing when running from a predator (in caveman times) or seeing your toddler fall into the lake. But a *chronic* release of cortisol has the opposite effect over time: It suppresses our immune system, decreases memory, and causes bone and muscle loss. And in the classroom? A study done by Clancy Blair, professor of applied psychology at

New York University, concluded that high cortisol levels decreased executive functions. Specifically, Blair states, "Detriments to executive function—as opposed to, say, low general mental ability—are the critical link tying high cortisol to low academic ability" (Blair, 2012, p. 66).

According to Sian Beilock (2011), the decrease in executive functioning is likely the result of the impact stress has on working memory. Working memory (short-term memory: what enables you to hold a phone number in your mind or a grocery list) is finite and different with each person—some people have high levels, some low. In general, the more working memory a person has, the better he or she will do on cognitive tasks such as problem solving and reasoning.

However, working memory is also where ruminations take place: When a person is stressed, working memory is thus occupied by worries. That stress can either be unrelated to the test *(Will I be hit today?)* or about the task at hand (anxiety about a test). The more anxiety one has, the less cognitive skills for the task. Indeed, Beilock and her colleagues discovered that when people with a normally high amount of working memory are exposed to anxiety, their ability to perform tasks matches that of someone with a lower amount of working memory.

Interestingly, Beilock (2011) found that students who spend 10 minutes expressing their thoughts and feelings about the test prior to the test achieved as much as a 7% increase in the outcome. Beilock writes, "Expressing concerns gives people some insight into the source of their stress, allowing them to reexamine the situation such that the tendency to worry during the actual stressful situation (and the resulting disruption of working memory) is limited" (p. 28). Writing about one's fears seems to help people reduce their anxiety and thus free up more working memory. An adaptation of her intervention is listed below.

Intervention 5.2: Journal for Test Success

Before administering your next exam, or perhaps before students take the SATs, have them write about their test fears for 10 minutes. What are their thoughts and feelings about the test they are about to take? How do they feel emotionally and physically? What have they done to prepare? What can they do to calm their stress? The more awareness you can prompt, the more likely students will come to the conclusion their stress is somewhat overexaggerated: that their parents truly won't kill them, that they are perfectly capable, and that the world isn't about to end. The more insight developed, the less anxiety experienced and, as Beilock found, the greater their chances for test success. Bottom line: If students have test anxiety, have them journal for 10 minutes about their fears before the test.

Long-term memory is also affected by stress. When under stress, the hippocampus decreases in size and subsequently loses the ability to remember. As a result, if a stressed student studies the night before a test, her recall the following day will be limited. In total, with the combination hippocampus inhibition (long-term memory) and executive function compromise (working/short-term memory), stress completely disrupts the optimal neural pathways for learning.

Stress comes from many sources: family, environment, economic status, poor nutrition, social anxieties, and more. But you can help by continuing to teach to the self and by maintaining a calm and nurturing environment in your classroom (see Chapter 8). When you reach the self, stress levels decrease, learning becomes available, and teens' confidence is bolstered, which then further decreases stress, increases learning, and the cycle continues. Below are several interventions to help you decrease stress levels in your students, thereby reaching their self and raising their cognitive capacities.

Intervention 5.3: Meditation and/or Focused Breathing

Studies on meditation, focused attention, and mindfulness have all shown remarkable benefits to the brain and body. For instance, meditation increases gray matter in the brain regions associated with memory, sense of self, empathy, and stress. In addition, hippocampus gray matter density increased and amygdala gray matter decreased (opening up PFC ability) (Bhanoo, 2011).

Indeed, schools have incorporated mindfulness into daily routines with profound effects including increased executive functions and reduced stress, anxiety, and poor behavior (Vega, 2012). Just what is mindfulness, you wonder? And how can you begin to reap its benefits? For starters, shift from a "do now" approach to a "be here" approach. Have signals that are meant to refocus your teens' attention to the here and now—such as a musical note or bell tone. This can be the prompt signaling the time to stop, quiet the mind, and relax. When prompted in this manner you are making clear the intention to focus. This skill doesn't just come; it is developed through practice. Then, walk them through the process of mindfulness/meditation. Instruct them to sit still, quiet their minds, and focus on something (a thought, feeling, sound, object) and to just let go while they strive to maintain focused attention. If giggles ensue, let them. Teens are apt to turn their nervousness at trying something new into laughter. But when you continue regardless, you are strengthening their ability to concentrate and relax, helping them tune into the task at hand and harness the power of their cognition. Meditation (discussed again in Chapter 7) can help quiet the mind, reduce stress, and increase focus. What could be a better state for taking a test? Tools to control their anxiety by harnessing the power of their minds can be used with or without you. They are self-empowering tools students will use for a lifetime.

Intervention 5.4: Stay on Task

Teaching students how to stay focused and to control their impulses calms the anxiety associated with completing a task. In Mischel's marshmallow study (see Chapter 4), the children who thought of ways to distract themselves from eating the treat were more likely to delay gratification for 18 minutes. But if they were *unable* to distract themselves, children became vulnerable to temptation in less than a minute. Mischel suggests that if we can control the contents of working memory (what we hold in consciousness for a short amount of time), then we can help attenuate distractions and stay on task (Tough, 2012).

This finding has large implications for your students' success in the classroom and at home. Mischel's follow up analyses showed a statistically significant difference in the social, career, health, and emotional lives of the two groups studied (those who could delay gratification and those who couldn't). One way to help students reduce stress by staying on task is to have them write down their task, their possible distractions, and their methods for staying on task. For example, *turn off the cell phone until I read 30 pages, then reward myself with a phone call to a friend.* This particular technique also strengthens the "planning ahead" and impulse control functions so tenuous at this age.

Intervention 5.5: Be a Dopamine Dispenser

Dopamine, the neurotransmitter associated with pleasure, also stimulates the PFC, specifically, executive functions. Dopamine, and other chemicals, carry electrical impulses from one neuron to another. Without this help, neurons wouldn't be as efficient in wiring together to form connections. The connections form a network that represents information learned. The stronger the network, the better your memory for it.

Why not become a dopamine dispenser? How? Let's say a student is late for your classroom . . . *again.* Here are two different ways to handle the situation. You could *react:*

"Sam, unbelievable! You're late again! This is totally unacceptable!"

Or, you could *respond* with eye contact and a smile:

"Welcome Sam, we were getting worried. Please take a seat, turn to page 38 and join us."

Does the welcoming response feel wrong to you? Do you feel as though your student needs admonishment? Before you answer, consider this: When a student is confronted with positive emotions—support, validation, empathy—his or her brain releases dopamine. Dopamine promotes attention, memory, comprehension, and impulse control.

Tips for dopamine dispensing include: Learn your roster for each class within the first 48 hours, if possible. Use names to greet students with a smile and eye contact as often as possible. Positively phrase instructions: "Hey Tara, show me those walking feet, please." Use humor, the ultimate dopamine dispenser, to deal with minor incidents. Quite often, adults seem as if they are all business and too serious. Let your teens see that you can take a joke and offer one just like they can.

Teacher Illustration 5.5: Dispensing Dopamine

Karen Williams, English Teacher at Indian Hills High School in Franklin Lakes, NJ

When Ms. Williams is speaking to her ninth-grade classes, she is very good at keeping their attention. However ninth graders are extremely social and often start to talk among themselves and can begin to disrupt others from listening. They can distract.

Instead of shushing them, or yelling, or saying "Quiet," or disciplining the students who are talking, she uses a very simple technique. She quietly says to the student or students, "Is everything all right back there? Are you ok?" The student response is immediate. They usually respond, "Yes" and quiet down and continue to listen to Karen. The students know what is going on, but no one has been disciplined or embarrassed. She shows concern instead of disapproval. Works like a charm!

Dispense Dopamine

Smile

Make eye contact

Say hello by name

Be nice

Put a positive spin on comments rather than a negative one

Have a positive disposition

Compliment effort and motivation

Learn the roster in 48 hours

Positive social interactions are what cause the release of dopamine! Furthermore, dopamine decreases the stress hormone cortisol. Cortisol is not our friend in the classroom. Dopamine is. The more you release it in your students' brains, the greater the chances of their learning, feeling confident, and feeling connected to school.

Intervention 5.6: Tap Into the Right Side of the Brain

When you turn down the left side (analytical, linear, logical) aspects of your brain, the right side is able to become more active. The right brain is where creative juices flow, opening new pathways for transformation. H. G. Wells, the famous English science fiction writer, observed his two sons playing with miniature figures and realized they were working out their problems through their creative play. Today, play therapy is a popular technique used to release the stress, anxiety, and fear associated with past experiences.

Thus, if you want to make change happen or you find yourself in a power struggle with a very clever 12-year-old, help her to access her creative skills. Move away from a strictly left-side logical approach by tapping into the right side of the brain with a creative activity. For instance, pull out some art supplies, sit down, and have a chat while coloring. You may find your discussion far more successful.

An Einstein Illustration

Einstein played the violin when faced with a challenging task at work. He often played in his kitchen late at night, ruminating over complicated scientific problems and potentials, until finally he would exclaim, "I've got it!" And, as if by magic, the answer to his problem would come to him in the middle of his musical endeavor (Robinson, 2009).

Intervention 5.7: Scaffold

Chapter 3 discusses scaffolding. Scaffolding enables for faster consolidation of material and less stress, so use it accordingly and allow stress to slip away.

Intervention 5.8: Improve Self-Control

When teens use coping skills to regulate their responses to stress, they exhibit one type of self-control: Instead of just reacting to a situation, they employ strategies such as counting to 10, taking a deep breath, or walking away. This self-control is an important part of the maturation process but is not always properly cultivated. As a result, students can become impulsive or irritable, or worse.

A study conducted by Hay and Meldrum (2010) found self-control (and parenting style) to be important to successful navigation of bullying situations. In fact, high self-control diminished the harmful effects of victimization for both self-harm and thoughts of suicide (Baird, 2010). Developing self-control skills in your students can help them regulate emotions and better manage difficult or potentially harmful situations.

Self-control development begins in the early years, but if you have students who still exhibit trouble inhibiting their impulses, you can help them increase their self-control. First, help them notice that they are impulsive; tap into their self-reflective minds. Point out situations where they may have reacted instinctively rather than responsively. Second, come alongside and think of ways to work on control: Help them develop strategies that feel manageable to them (deep breathing, etc.). Finally, provide an exercise (or two!) such as counting to 10 before moving when the bell rings between classes to reset the impulse buttons to be more relaxed and less reactive.

Teacher Illustration 5.8: Self-Control Sticky Notes

Jennifer Weber, Instructor, Teacher Education, South Dakota State University, Brookings, SD

One of my middle school students had a very difficult time with blurting out off-topic questions and inappropriate stories. I tried many unsuccessful strategies such as standing near him, reminding him to raise his hand, and encouraging him to think before he raised his hand. He was a very social middle school student, and I knew his ultimate currency was being with his friends in the classroom.

So, I decided to place three light bulb sticky notes on the top of his desk at the start of his class period every day. Every time he spoke out in class or raised his hand to tell/ask something, I would take one of the light bulbs away. When all three bulbs were gone, he would have to be quiet for the remainder of the period. If he ran out of bulbs and still blurted out remarks, he would have to spend the rest of his class period in the hallway outside my room if there was a monitor there, or in a quiet room in the office, separating him entirely from his friends.

At first, his light bulbs disappeared at record speed, but slowly, he came to recognize the consequences. He really needed to think before he used a bulb. He started raising his hand, sometimes putting it back down because he "thought better" of his choice to speak at that time, knowing he only had three opportunities all class period. This process really taught him the self-control he needed to make it through an entire class period without derailing the structure of the course.

Intervention 5.9: Assess the Stress!

Check in with your population and find out exactly how they are feeling. Create a quick survey yourself. Include the following five questions to gain insight into how stressed your students are, how they deal, and to whom they can turn. Remember to tell them that their answers are kept confidential.

On a scale of 1 to 10, how stressed are you (10 being off-the-charts-totally-stressed out)?

List the top five things that stress you out.

List the people to whom you can turn for help (parent, teacher, coach, counselor, etc.).

List one to three ways your stress limits your abilities in life, work, play, friends, etc.

How do you manage your stress?

If any of their answers concern you, speak with them or consult with a school counselor under rules of confidentiality.

> The more successful parenting style found in Hay and Meldrum's (2010) study is referred to as "authoritative." It involves being a good listener, providing scaffolding, showing and earning respect, and showing a genuine interest in the lives of teens without crowding their sense of space. Sound like anything you've been reading so far?

Teacher Illustration 5.9: Validate the Stress for Academic Success

Paula Prentis, School Social Work Intern, Metropolitan Corporate Academy, Brooklyn, NY, 1996

When I was a social work intern at an alternative high school, I learned firsthand how stress and real life problems affect academics and potential life success. I worked with teens whose primary concern was daily survival. From the pregnant students to the ones in gangs, from the girlfriend ruled by her hit-man uncle to the boy who desperately wanted to be a warlock (a man who practices witchcraft), I had my hands full. I felt overwhelmed at first, not knowing how I could help these extremely real but unusual factors that kept my group of students from attending to their work. As a start, I made a "contract" with each one. They had to keep a journal, which I would read on my own time (and make comments if they wanted), but the time we had together needed to be divided into two parts: First, they would be able to tell me of their most pressing issues. Second, we would spend time focusing on how to work through the issues so academics could find a place in their worlds. The resistances were palpable, but in time with authenticity and consistency, my students handed in their journals, spoke about what kept them from academics, and eventually provided me with their ideas on how to manage their academics on top of all their other issues. I wish I could say that every one of them turned into a success story, but I can't. I do know that I was able to shift their consciousnesses enough to contemplate their lives in the context of school. They were overwhelmed with emotions and survival, so cognition and academics had no real meaning in their worlds. By helping them vent their stories, structure their time and focus, they were able to shift gears and begin to imagine the possibilities.

NEUROPLASTICITY: THE ROLE OF EXPERIENCES

Each experience that we have not only impacts brain functions, but also shapes brain structure. Understanding the relationship between past experiences and brain functions allows us the opportunity to mindfully shape our brains in the direction of our choosing. Thus, when we manage emotions such as stress, we are not only creating better learning opportunities in the present, but also creating neural pathways that will actually shape our futures.

Repeated experiences at a very young age cause us to think and feel a certain way and contribute to our self-perceptions. Remember the diagram from Chapter 4.

The cyclical nature of our thoughts, emotions, and experiences.

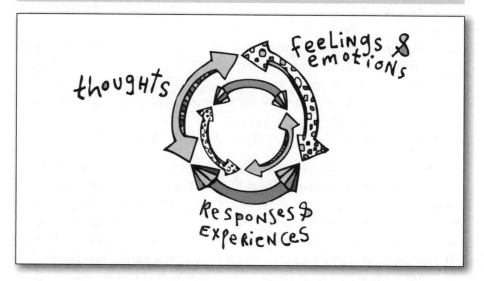

Now let's look at an illustration that indicates what is happening at a cellular level.

Synapses shown here are firing based on repeated thought patterns.

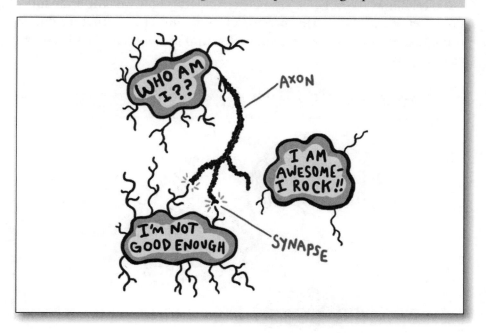

When we have an experience

- Neurons fire
- Genes "express" themselves (produce protein)
- Myelin production is stimulated (the slick surface on which signals travel along the axon of a nerve cell—the slicker the myelin, the faster the signal)
- The number of synapses increases—thereby strengthening the connections between neurons.
- Voila! Our brains have changed. (Norden, 2007)

Much of our personality, character, morality, and resilience have been shaped—on a cellular level—from our experiences. For example, when trauma sabotages the life of a young tyke, the subsequent stress response diminishes the potential for resilience. On the other hand, positive parental influences support the nervous system and increase resilience (Siegel, 2010). Young children can't do much about their early experiences, but they can learn very much about who they are as a result of them. This increased self-awareness is the first step toward change. In fact, the stronger a person's ability to acknowledge reality, even when unpleasant, the less likely the more primitive defenses (refer to Chapter 3) are to develop.

Moreover, by focusing attention on new thoughts and feelings, we can literally shift where our cells strengthen and thus how well the brain functions (see illustration). This process of changing brain structure due to thoughts, behavior, environment, and neural processes is what is known as *neuroplasticity.*

Synapses here are firing based on a new way of thinking.

Early abuse on youngsters (bullying, parental neglect, repeated punishments) can permanently damage their DNA causing premature aging and even taking years off their lives. "Researchers examined telomeres—genetic material at the tips of chromosomes—in more than 100 young children . . . They found that those who had been exposed to childhood violence had shorter telomeres, which can have deleterious effects on the immune system causing many health problems. Of note, smoking, obesity, and mental problems can all permanently shorten telomeres" ("Health Scare of the Week," 2012).

Through neuroplasticity, we have the ability to wire new connections based on what we decide to think or do or focus on in any given situation. We simply need to become more aware and focus our thoughts. Chapter 4 explores the importance of becoming more aware to regulate our emotions and behaviors, and this is yet another reason why such awareness is so critical. Awareness allows for choice: choice on how to both respond to a situation and to direct the formation of healthy neural pathways. Awareness, by definition, means becoming more in touch with the self. Thus, when you increase awareness, you reach and build the self.

When Students Are Tired in Class

The following true story is told by 48-year-old Jock Patterson from San Francisco, CA, reflecting on an experience from boarding school. "Where I went to school, everyone sat around in a circle to discuss topics. It is a great method, but also one in which the teacher can see everyone. One kid in class was dozing off. The teacher picked up a book and slammed it down on the table in front of the kid and then screamed at him, 'I will not tolerate sleeping in *my* class!' We were all frozen in fear. Another time one of my teachers approached me after a class and said, 'Jock, you look tired today. Is everything okay?'" This begs the questions: Which student's self was affirmed? Which was shamed?

Our brains literally fire electrical impulses that wire neurons together based on our thoughts about our experiences and our emotions. This is why the way that we frame experiences is so important to our students' health. For instance, when a child says, "I don't know" instead of confirming their self-doubt with a "Not good, Mr. Smith; the information was in your homework," make "I don't know" a positive learning experience.

"Fantastic! You don't know! That's why we are here! To discover and find out! I'm glad you let me know that, now I know what I need to teach you. What an opportunity!" Students are often taught to be ashamed of the state of "not knowing." What if we were to welcome it as a sign of direction and opportunity?

Because of neuroplasticity, and the opportunities it provides, let's help students realize that they are who they are based on the thoughts they have about themselves. Those thoughts are often largely based on the past. The past is over. Every day, because of neuroplasticity, students have the power (as do we!) to create new thoughts and experiences to catapult them into a future of success. Thus, this begs the question, what can we do to increase their motivation to make those changes and succeed?

IMPROVING MOTIVATION

All human behavior is motivated. Indeed, Chapter 3 demonstrated that acting out and other defenses seen in your classrooms are often motivated by fear. Students behave in a certain manner to protect themselves from potential hurt or disappointment: That is the motivation driving their behaviors. You may no longer read this book, but it doesn't mean you are not motivated. It means you are more motivated to do something else! The question becomes, what is the drive behind your motivation? And then, how can we use that information to bring your motivation back to reading this book? Likewise, your student, Garrett, may be completely unmotivated in school. What is the drive behind Garrett's motivation and how can we use that information about Garrett to bring his motivation back to participating in school?

Motivation falls into two categories: intrinsic and extrinsic. Intrinsic motivation comes from within—you do something simply because you enjoy the process of doing it, such as raising children, playing a sport, or volunteering at the local shelter. Extrinsic motivation comes from the outside—you do something because you anticipate a reward, such as fame, prestige, money, or even power. Intrinsic and extrinsic motivation are two different pathways to tread when trying to motivate students. However, it is intrinsic motivation that is more powerful, purposeful, and long-lasting. In fact, it is the only form of motivation that fits the demanding and multivaried needs of our current environment and global marketplace (Pink, 2009).

Intrinsic motivation stems from the knowledge we have about our selves—our inner core/container—and the subsequent drives, passions, and purpose that stem from that knowledge. Our self-perceptions and self-awareness intrinsically motivate us to either succeed or fail at school, at work, in relationships, and in love. Imagine 12-year-old Lucinda. She thinks of herself as the next Mia Hamm. Is she more likely to (motivated to!) practice soccer drills each day or blow them off? If Pedro imagines himself building robots for NASA, is he more likely to do his science homework? Conversely, if Kendra thinks she is a horrible math student, what will she continue to prove to you? To herself? What do your students aspire to be? Teaching to the self allows us to both build their confidence and connect their beliefs about who they can be, creating the intrinsic motivation necessary for learning. As you provide the self skills that nourish the seeds of passion and interest, motivation grows.

However, our current educational (indeed cultural) climate focuses more on extrinsic rewards, the "carrot and the stick" so to speak. Countless studies (Pink, 2009) have found that this focus has some severely negative effects. In one well-known study, Lepper, Greene, and Nisbett (1973) studied extrinsic motivation on preschool children. They worked with a group of nursery school-aged students who all loved to draw pictures and divided them into three groups. The first group was told they would receive an award for drawing. The second group was given a choice to draw or not, and then given an award *after* they drew (they did not expect the award). The third group neither expected nor received an award. Two weeks later, which groups were motivated to draw when provided the opportunity? Groups 2 and 3. Which group was no longer as interested? Group 1. Why? The prizes had taken the fun, the intrinsic motivation, out of the equation.

Daniel Pink, in his book *Drive* (2009), discusses the critical need to "update" our motivational systems from extrinsic to intrinsic:

> Traditional "if-then" rewards can give us less of what we want: They can extinguish intrinsic motivation, diminish performance, crush creativity, and crowd out good behavior. They can also give us more of what we don't want: They can encourage unethical behavior, create addictions, and foster short-term thinking. These are the bugs in our current operating system. (p. 220)

But what do we do from day one in school? We set up reward systems through which they can get stars or smiley faces if they behave/perform a certain way. We give them grades, for various reasons, but one of those reasons is to challenge students to achieve *better* grades (extrinsic motivators). To use Pink's analogy, we are using outdated software on a sophisticated new operating system. That old software is based upon a flawed assumption that all challenge motivates us. *Challenge only motivates you **if** you are confronted by problems that you feel you are reasonably capable of solving and that **interest** you.* Both of these factors have to do with the self. Both of these factors tap intrinsic motivation.

Let's explore the first factor of the self: feeling capable. When the mind believes that it cannot meet a challenge, the self can feel threatened: It will fear the challenge. In fact, that fear is compounded if you are 13 years old, and your performance is based on your result—such as your grade—and not your effort. Thus, when we challenge kids to do better in school, many of them are feeling *threatened* at their very core. Self-doubt saturates the container walls. Time and time again, when report cards or tests occur, we are making teens feel worse about themselves—*not motivating them.* In fact, for some, we are causing them to want to run and hide, and eventually to *drop out.*

Or even worse, drop out of life, like *Race to Nowhere* (Abeles, 2010) so clearly showed us. What if that child had a solid inner core? What if her self-concept was more than her grades? What if she had been judged on her efforts and not her results? Students need to feel capable of performance before they will ever feel motivated by it. Feeling capable is a component of the self. (More on the importance of focusing on effort can be found in Chapter 8.)

Are Grades Motivating?

When competition is fierce, motivation can actually break down. Imagine you are a C student placed in a room with Mr. and Mrs. A. Student. You are to take a state test. How is your motivation now? Research has shown that the C student will do worse on this test than if she had taken the test on her own: Simply being reminded that she is inferior by comparison brings down her performance (Beilock, 2011; Tough, 2012). Competition is only motivating for those who think they can win/do well. For those who don't, it's discouraging and defeating. *Self*-defeating (Combs, 2010).

Second to the idea that *one must feel capable of solving the challenge* is the idea that one must find some *level of interest in the challenge.* This interest is what motivates us to rise to the challenge: to excel at our work or meet a deadline. We act not on mere information but on our personal interests, including our feelings and beliefs about that information. In order to increase our level of interest, students need to have a sense of self—a spark to ignite motivation. (More on motivation can be found in Chapter 9.)

A sense of self increases interest, which increases motivation.

Personal Meaning and Interest

To illustrate the importance of personal meaning on interest, let's pretend that you are sitting in the teacher's lounge next to two other teachers having a conversation. At first, the teachers are discussing which textbook they plan on using for health this semester. Since you don't teach health, you pay very little attention. Next, the conversation turns to some trouble they might have in getting students to participate in an outdoor activity, so you begin to eavesdrop because you sometimes have participation issues in your classroom and would like to know how other teachers handle it. Next, they mention that Justin might be difficult to engage. This interests you more because you have a Justin in one of your classes that is just baffling you: He disrupts class in the most subtle and annoying ways. Could it be the same person? Your interest becomes totally locked and loaded though when they debate involving the parents, Mr. and Mrs. Larkin. Justin Larkin? So it is the same person! Other people are finding him difficult as well! *Complete interest.* Why? Because you have *emotions* attached to the situation, which you didn't when the teachers were talking about possible health books. *The closer the personal meaning, the more your interest was piqued.*

Thus, to help students tap into their intrinsic motivation incorporate curriculum that allows them to build their identities and therefore connect with topics at hand (students will find little personal meaning with a vague identity). Below are a few interventions to inspire motivation—both intrinsic and extrinsic—within your students.

> **Bottom line:** *Help students tap into their sense of self, and you will help them discover their intrinsic motivation.*

Intervention 5.10: Put Information in Context to Increase the Level of Interest

Students continually wonder, *Why does history matter? How will math help me?* But until they have a sense of what does matter to them, no answer will suffice, and rote information is simply pruned after the test. To help them self-motivate, provide the connection between lesson and life application. This is why project-based learning (PBL) and service learning (SL) have gained such momentum. A positive correlation exists between these pedagogies and the self: As students work on one, they feel more confident in the other. (To access a variety of lesson plans that include both PBL and SL, please visit yourselfseries.com/teachers/.)

Some ideas to motivate students by making traditional subjects more personally meaningful are below.

- Suggest to them, *since we are studying famous inventors of the 18th century, choose one who invented something that has meaning to you or has affected your life in some way. Provide the inventor's life history, why the invention is important to you, how you connect with the inventor's philosophies, and how the person helped the world.*
- Math may seem useless until you give everyone a bank account and have them add and subtract to it according to any number of activities you do in the classroom. Negotiation skills are honed as they debate the ability to purchase free time or homework exemptions from the "money" in their bank accounts.
- When reading English literature, have students write their reports as though they were the main character. Have them discuss how they felt when the main events happened and what they might have done differently. Or, have them create an analogy between the story and something that has personal relevance to them.
- In health class, have students make up recipes. With each ingredient, they must describe what nutrients are provided and how those nutrients help/hinder the body. Have them determine the caloric value of their recipe and thus, the activities in which they would need to participate to use those calories.

If we want students to understand and learn from Anne Frank, Einstein, Madame Bovary, or the Food and Drug Administration's (FDA) Plate, we need to help them connect the material to their own lives, and thus, their selves.

Intervention 5.11: Immediate Feedback

Mr. Taylor assigns an eight-page research paper on the Ottoman Empire. Students work harder than ever. Maddy, who has struggled in this class, stays on task because *you* taught her the antistress methods from the previous section. She turned off her cell phone and Facebook account for a week! Stressed, but relieved, she hands in her paper. Mr. Taylor has a family obligation over the weekend and doesn't return the graded papers for nearly 10 days. When he does, he has marked a 76 on Maddy's paper: but with no comments, no help as to how to improve. How does Maddy feel about her work? What has she learned?

If we want students to be excited about a project, to apply themselves, and to connect with the material, why make them wait for feedback that would benefit them if they received it immediately (at least before beginning the next unit)? "When you provide students with opportunities to apply learning—especially through authentic, personally meaningful activities—and then provide formative assessments and feedback throughout a unit, facts move from rote memory to become part of the memory bank" (Willis, 2011b). Often we assess work less effectively and efficiently than students' minds necessitate. The feedback that some teachers (not all!) currently provide does little to motivate and inform students as to their potentialities. The time lapse is disheartening to the student who has been taught that all that matters is the grade, rather than the material learned. Grades are a deterrent to success when not followed up with immediate, constructive, personally meaningful feedback that points students toward a next steps approach (Combs, 1997).

Intervention 5.12: Lay It on the Line

Another way to spur motivation is to have students "lay it on the line." Have them invest/predict/bet on their learning. Create a chart before they learn a unit on the Civil War. *What I know now/What I don't know/What I will learn/Why it matters to me (in relation to humanity, morality, history, etc.).* By writing it, they begin to incorporate it into who they are and they build executive functions—planning ahead, analyzing, prioritizing, reviewing. They begin to own their learning. Who else should own their learning if not they? (Jacobs, 2010; Willis, 2011a). Concurrently, allow students to work in groups so they can collaborate on their predictions and their findings. Through setting goals, trial and error, and rethinking possibilities, learning goes from a win-*lose* feeling to a win-*learn* experience. By laying it on the line, students become motivated, learning increases, and the neural networks consolidate for future application.

Intervention 5.13: Connect With Students' Style of Learning

After helping students make connections between the material and the self, another way to increase motivation is to help them connect with their style of learning. Often, you are asked to tailor teaching to meet your students' needs whether it be auditory, visual, kinesthetic, etc. Instead, empower students to take the controls and navigate their own course. Ask them to think about the different ways learning takes place: through sight, sound, movement, etc. What feels natural to them? What subjects are easiest for them to learn: ones that are more hands on (visual, kinesthetic) or perhaps ones that are more of a traditional lecture (auditory)? Introduce the concept that learning takes place via many different avenues, and what may be best for them can help them to reach their destination (topic comprehension) quicker. (However, as Daniel T. Willingham [2009] points out, altering your style of teaching to reach each student's individual learning strengths is not always optimal. Some subjects are best taught a certain way, which is why cognitive flexibility is important to obtain.)

A Word About Power Struggles

A teacher or principal (anyone, really) who feels that he or she needs to "show who's boss" will lose power in the eyes of others. But, you can give power (a motivator) without losing your own! Students don't want your power (they certainly don't want to teach your class!); they just want some of their own (Lavoie, 2013). To give power (and not lose yours) provide choices for your students: *you need to run for 25 minutes, would you like to do it around the track or baseball field?* Or, at home: *You need to feed the dog—you choose wet food or dry. Thanks.* If you find yourself involved in too many power struggles with students, look inward. After all, you're the one with the power—how are you using it? Be sure it is positive, helping you connect with students, rather than negative, such as punishments or acts that make your students feel shame or embarrassment. One teacher refuses to allow students to use the bathroom during her class. Another boasts that no student could possibly be as smart as she. These acts of authority are unnecessary and undermine the purpose of learning.

CHAPTER SUMMARY

Check In With Your Self

From the list below, put a check next to the category that you feel (and think!) you could confidently teach to your students tomorrow and tell them why it is important for them to know:

- Hippocampus
- Stress-reduction techniques
- Dopamine
- Executive functions
- Cortisol
- Working memory
- Neuroplasticity
- Amygdala
- Prefrontal cortex

Interventions

Teach basic brain anatomy and function

Journal for test success

Meditation and/or focused breathing

Stay on task

Be a dopamine dispenser

Tap into the right side of the brain

Scaffold

Improve self-control

Assess the stress

Put information into context

Immediate feedback

Lay it on the line

Connect with students' styles of learning

Activity: Decrease Stress and Increase Motivation

Situation	Goal	Intervention
Describe a situation you hope to improve.	What do you hope to achieve with the student?	Which intervention in the chapter will you use?
Lucinda frequently moans over her grades and seems unmotivated to apply herself.	*Less moaning and more motivation.*	*Immediate feedback* *Connect with style of learning*

Outcome
List the time frame and overall impressions.
Immediately, I made a concerted effort to grade papers in a timely fashion and allow students to rewrite accordingly so they could learn from mistakes. Lucinda read all my comments and worked hard on rewrites. I also noticed that she listened to music incessantly. I suggested she read her papers out loud so she could hear the logic and flow. She reported that this method was indeed helpful. Hearing the essay resonated with her more than merely reading it had.

Now construct a chart from your experience.

The Social Self: Consolidate the Self in the Social World

6

Students correctly understand, though adults appear not to, that socialization is the most intellectually demanding and morally important thing they will do in high school.

—Brooks (2011, p. 75)

WHAT YOU WILL LEARN IN THIS CHAPTER

This chapter reviews Step 5: Consolidate the self in the social world. In this chapter, you will learn how to

- Set a positive social tone in your classroom
- Develop social skills to aid in student collaboration
- Effectively utilize teamwork

SET A POSITIVE SOCIAL TONE IN YOUR CLASSROOM

In the past, society has taught social rules and expectations to its generations. Today, however, with the bombardment of media influences and the core family structure in flux, all coupled with the highest stress levels, suicide rates, medicinal therapies, and health concerns to date, the need to model, support, and teach appropriate social skills is more critical than ever.

Remember that, according to your students, school is primarily a social place. Learning is, for most, secondary. The majority of your students view school as either a time to connect with their friends or a social battlefield they need to survive each day. Indeed, providing skills to help them navigate those battles will ease their stress and bring them back to learning.

In this section, we discuss how you can make your classroom socially friendly while pursuing high academic standards. The suggestions below include: icebreakers, classroom set up and structure, classroom rules and consequences, expected behavior modeling, being available and approachable, and appropriate tone of voice.

Positive Social Tone 1: Icebreakers

Icebreakers demand connection and more clearly define a sense of self. Icebreakers insist that the self be present because they encourage personal involvement. Sitting alone at a desk, the student can easily drift into never-never land or silently criticize the fashion statement of the person sitting next to him or her. But with an icebreaker, such "head chatter" is not possible, and each individual is required to bring something of himself or herself to the table. Moreover, icebreakers are not academically challenging. Thus, the stress present from having to perform academically is temporarily abated while the self gains strength from being called to the present.

Many teachers have a set of icebreakers they use. If you are not someone who uses icebreakers, consider for a moment how different your class might be if you required your students to partake in such an activity. If stuck for ideas, search the Internet for exercises that you feel would work well with your students. Social connection increases the likelihood of student engagement and learning. No matter what product or activity you choose, remember that icebreakers can bring together a disparate group. We suggest using them at the beginning of the school year when the air can be thick with social anxiety, *or whenever you feel your class is disjointed or frustrated with each other.*

Example 6.1: Icebreakers

Divide your class into groups of three to five students. Have each group do a "go around": The first person introduces herself by first name and her talent/favorite hobby/favorite trip (you choose). The next person looks at her and says, "Your name is Maggy; you love photography. My name is Carlos and I love to travel." And so on. Once the smaller groups have completed this, have them merge with another group to make a larger group, and so on until the whole class is together. Doing so in small steps lessens anxiety and increases connections and confidence. What has this accomplished? For one: memory. Students will devise ways to remember, and they will even help each other—empathy. They will use eye contact, make connections, and tap into emotions. Have them list and discuss all the emotions they experienced. How did they manage their emotions? Did they recognize emotions in others?

Positive Social Tone 2:
Classroom Set Up and Structure

The traditional classroom set up shown here on the left in this diagram is a formation rarely seen or experienced again by your students as they head off to boardrooms and meetings, big and small, here and abroad.

This is an illustration of two methods of learning. On the left is the traditional teaching method, and on the right is the Harkness Learning Method.

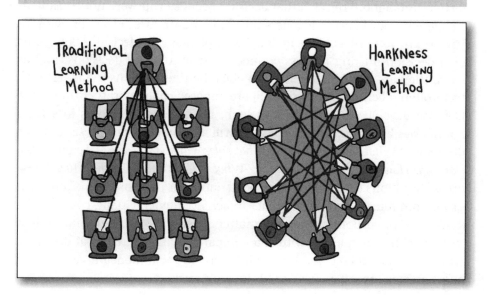

As such, why continue to always teach in this formation? Why not, when appropriate, teach in a circle or oval, such as the Harkness model shown here? When in an oval, students truly "see" each other and develop connections, compassion, and the courage to be who they are. The circular approach promotes community. As one student stated, "At Deerfield, English and history classes use the Harkness method. Each day we review what was read the night before in an open-discussion style. This is beneficial for students because it allows them to state their opinions on certain issues and to receive constructive responses from other classmates. I really enjoy these classes" (Doug Vallar, 16, Bedford, NY).

When a lesson is well suited for discussion among your students, have your students move their desks to form a large circle in your room (engaging their physical self in the process). You can even have prearranged days that you do this, or a prearranged signal that such a formation will be necessary. Of course, not every lesson is ideally suited for the Harkness method. When you are writing vast amounts of information on the chalkboard or using a Smartboard, you may not want students' backs facing you. In these circumstances, a more traditional structure may be more appropriate, or if your room size allows, consider a horseshoe shape, a terrific blend of both formations.

Positive Social Tone 3: Classroom Rules and Consequences

Have you ever been excluded in a decision-making situation and, as a form of retaliation, rejected that decision because you were not consulted? Imagine if your team of teachers adopted a new course of action without you. Might you feel a bit less inclined to implement the decision? Being part of a decision-making process connects people to those decisions, and as such, they are much more likely to abide by the decisions made. Like us, teens often rebel against norms that are imposed *on* them, rather than rules that are developed *with* them. As such, include your students in setting boundaries in the classroom. The self will automatically be present in this discussion: *What do I think is fair? What rules will keep me safe and promote my learning? How will that rule affect me? What if I don't abide by that rule?* These are all questions that address the social nature of the classroom: You are a group that must cooperate together to achieve a goal. Finally, consider the student in the corporate arena in a matter of years. Do we want that student to *demand* things happen within a company, making unilateral decisions while expecting a collaborative atmosphere? Or, will modeling a collective effort now be more beneficial to his future career?

Teacher Illustration 6.1: Collaborative Rule Building

Amy Smith, English Teacher, Ramapo High School, Franklin Lakes, NJ

I wanted my tenth-grade English class to be committed to writing good essays. Over the course of a week, I distributed various essays from former students and had my students evaluate them and give them grades. Each day, we would discuss the essays and the grades they thought they deserved. We discussed strong points and weak points of each essay and compiled a list of the aspects that made them strong. By the end of the week, the students had compiled a list of characteristics that were apparent in an "A" essay.

On Monday, I wrote the attributes for the rubric on the board. I then asked them to assign points for each attribute, making them total 100 points. They had to decide what were the most important attributes of an essay and assign them the most points. After that, we discussed what would gain all the points under each attribute, and then, on a sliding scale, how many points would be removed for failings in each category.

The reality was they were spot on with their decisions, and all I had to do was type it into a form that guided them for every essay they wrote. I used that rubric each time I graded their essays, assigning points in each category. Their grade was a composite of those points, and they could clearly see where their strengths and weaknesses were. Most important, this was not something imposed upon them. It came from them, and because of that, there were few arguments about their grades. Also, it told them where they needed to work. When we did peer reviewing, everyone was on the same page. Everyone understood the aspects of the rubric. They owned their essays.

Moreover, think carefully about discipline. In a Texas study, kids who were harshly disciplined and/or expelled were more likely to repeat a grade, never return, or drop out than students who were not disciplined in the same way (Shah, 2012). What will your students perceive as harsh? By involving them in the rule setting and the philosophy behind certain rules, your students will be less likely to view a rule as too demanding or unfair. Setting rules and procedures also enforces responsibility taking—a major social skill.

Teacher Illustration 6.2: Student Rule Enforcement

Victor Manielly, Education Specialist, Durham, NC

Students need opportunities to interact with their peers, develop social skills, fail often, and grow through their experiences in the face of their peers (who, in their eyes, matter way much more than adults).

In my work, if a student blew it or did something really disrespectful, my approach was to take the power out of my hands and place it in the hands of the class. The offense was presented, with the accused front and center, and I would present an option, through a voting process, to either convict or acquit, with some reasonable sentence if the prior was chosen. Then a silent vote was collected on small sheets of paper, and peers decided fate. This proved to be very powerful stuff, and the times that I felt justice was not served I can count on one finger.

None of this comes easily. To say making any of this happen takes a great deal of patience, time in the trenches, holding tough consistently to expectations, and having big ole ears is a monstrous understatement. But students know the teachers that care enough to put the time and effort into finding them where they are, and though the appreciation is often deeply disguised, it's there.

Positive Social Tone 4: Model Expected Behavior

Your students are often living through a social climate in which they feel as though they might want to rip out *their* hair—so instead, they often act out, making you feel as though you want to rip out *your* hair! Modeling how you expect them to behave in the midst of stress and difficult times is critical. Telling your students they must act well while you lash out at them sends a message of disconnect: *One set of rules for me, and one set of rules for you.* The self is better served through connection: *This is how we all behave.* Therefore, avoid sarcasm, put-downs, ridicule, gossip, negativity, eye rolling, blaming, rudeness, etc. Promote positive and proactive thoughts and actions, compliments, compassion, empathy, and community. (The previous chapter on the cognitive self discussed being a dopamine dispenser. This is an example of how to be one.)

Teacher Illustration 6.3: The Story Behind the Story

Tara Brown, Learner's Edge Consulting, Nashville, TN

In working with kids, 99% of the time, there is always a "story behind the story." When a child loses his head in class, appears to be rude or disrespectful, or any number of behaviors adults deem inappropriate, often if we (the adults) can take a few more seconds before making assumptions (and having a knee jerk reaction) and approach the child and model compassion, empathy, calm under pressure, and an openness to see that child as the individual that they are, then we will often open the door to getting a clearer view of the real story that caused the child to act the way she did. Adults just need to be motivated to find the story behind the story.

In short, when adults open their hearts and have the sincere desire to lead with empathy and compassion, it is often all a child needs to lower defenses, communicate honestly, and embrace the positive modeling being done at that crucial time of course correction.

Positive Social Tone 5: Be Available and Approachable

To connect with teens, speak their language. The language of today is increasingly digital. Ignoring this reality is like ignoring that some students speak English as a second language. Allow students to ask questions and clarify expectations through e-mail, or another appropriate digital service. For many of your students, communication this way will be easier because of their familiarity with it. The less stressed they feel about contacting you, the more likely the connection remains open and feels safe.

Check In With Your Self

On a scale of 1 to 10, 10 being the go-to teacher when times are tough, how approachable do you feel you are to your students? What makes you feel that way? How could you be considered more approachable? Can you think of one way this week you can increase your approachability?

An eighth-grade physics teacher at a private school goes out of his way to e-mail his class of "engineers," to keep them up to date on assignments and to make sure they were safe after a recent storm (Super-storm Sandy, 2012). Kyla Spence is in his class: "It makes me feel like he cares to teach us, not like it's his job: like he really wants to. It makes me want to give to him the same kind of effort he gives to us."

"We appreciate when you connect with us in our worlds such as the teacher who provided us with extra help using Xbox and Skype" (Student discussing her desires on NBC Education Nation with Ann Curry, September 2011).

In addition, a suggestion box placed in your classroom that encourages students to ask questions or make comments anonymously allows for more tentative students to voice their concerns. Acknowledge comments and create open discussions so others may share how they feel on the issue.

If time allows, consider anonymously thanking students who contributed their thoughts—all thoughts. This validates the self and promotes further connections. Recognition acknowledges their significance. Not acknowledging someone, as in repeatedly not calling on someone who eagerly raises her hand each day, extinguishes potential connection.

Positive Social Tone 6: Consider Your Tone of Voice

We are social creatures, and picking up on the subtleties of communication is a significant part of our survival. *What* you say is almost less important to the brain's intake centers than *how* you say it. Your tone of voice speaks volumes. To a student, a slight variation in pitch can mean the difference between receiving direction and refusing instruction. As such, be aware of the tone you use with your students and, most important, make students aware of the tone of voice they are using. For example, you might respond to a student with, "Wow, that was an insightful question John, but from the tone of your voice, I am wondering if you are frustrated." This teaches them that they are sending messages not just with their words, but with their tones. Awareness of this avenue of communication is a vital social skill.

TOP SOCIAL SKILLS

If you were asked to design a set of global competencies that students should be taught, where on that list would you put *the ability to get along well with others?* We think it would be pretty close to the top. The ability to get along with others is a leading indicator of how successful one will be at teamwork (discussed in the next section). In this section, we discuss two key elements necessary before teamwork can effectively take place: communication and cooperation. Ways to develop these skills and how they fit into your students' lives are listed below.

Social Skill 1: Effective Communication

Communication is one of the primary social skills necessary for survival on the job, in a relationship, in public, and in private. If students are going to feel and be successful working in groups, having debates, conversing over the Internet, or handling conflict, they must acquire effective verbal and nonverbal skills of communication. Students need to be aware of how well they present to others and also how well they listen (a critical yet often overlooked component of communication). As a key part of our social selves, learning how to communicate respectfully and effectively will promote the ability to get along well with others.

By making the following principles of communication a habit in your classroom, you will proactively squash the seeds of misunderstanding while cultivating the social self.

> **Check In With Your Self**
>
> Is your communication style effective? Do you feel you explain yourself well? Listen with the intent to understand instead of with the intent to respond? Do people respond to you the way you had hoped?

Communication Is a Two-Way Street

Communication is a two-way street where one person expresses and the other person shows he or she is listening by responding accordingly. Teach students that, as in soccer, if a teammate ignores your pass, you would likely become frustrated. But when a teammate goes out of his way to trap the ball, even if the pass was not accurate, and passes back, then you are more likely to feel a connection. Likewise communication is a "team" effort—individuals work together to promote a positive experience. Thus, ignoring the efforts of others to communicate and to connect is both frustrating and disrespectful, just as ignoring a pass in soccer would be.

Moreover, listening is a skill that requires practice, but too often a skill that receives little attention. Today, teens have many distractions that can keep them from listening well (texts, social stresses, school pressures, etc.), and as such, they need to be more cognizant of their listening skills. One strategy to help ensure that your students are developing these listening skills is to occasionally require them to repeat what you or another student has said—exactly. Your students may find that this is often a difficult task to achieve.

Intervention 6.1: Telephone

Discuss the game Telephone with your students—the game they played when they were younger in which one person whispered something in a person's ear, and that person, in turn, whispered it to the person next to him until the final person in the chain blurted out the phrase she heard that was usually ridiculously different from the original phrase. Each person only had one chance to whisper the phrase. The main concept here: "If you don't listen well, things can get pretty messed up rather quickly." Although those mistakes may have been silly when playing Telephone, they can be the cause of many misunderstandings as you get older. Discuss where the difficulties lie with Telephone: Is it the phrase, the person speaking the message, or the receiver who is at fault? E-mail and texts don't reflect voice modulations and this can confuse intent and meaning. The game Telephone allows us to see that we must both articulate well and listen well for proper communication to take place.

Words Are Powerful: Choose Carefully

Miscommunication usually stems from poor listening skills (addressed above) and/or from poorly chosen words. "I hate you!" is significantly different from "I hate what you just did." One attacks the self;

the other criticizes an action. The former shuts down cognition. The latter at least keeps the lines of communication open. Encourage students to find the right words to express their feelings, even if they may struggle at times; script responses for your students if necessary. Help them find the right words that respectfully express what they wish to say. Speaking well is a developed skill just as writing well. We don't hesitate to offer suggestions with their written words. Providing scripts for them when they are feeling motivated to react, rather than respond, helps mitigate potential mishaps.

For example, if one of your students keeps blurting out statements such as, "That's so stupid; it doesn't make any sense" during your lessons, help that student find a more constructive way to voice his concerns. "Sumil, when you use words like that, it can set a negative tone in the classroom. When you are feeling frustrated, could you say to me, 'Miss Reynolds, I'm getting confused. I don't understand what you just said'?"

Encourage Students to Use Names and Make Eye Contact

When names are used, a deeper connection is made between individuals. Both selves are called to be more present. Often you may hear students say, "I agree with what she said." Ask that students use names: "I agree with you, Regina." In addition, ask that students make eye contact with the person they are addressing. The age of computers has severely depersonalized communication. By promoting eye contact and the use of names, you are repersonalizing communication and thus promoting connection between students.

Consider Nonverbal Communication

Body language is important as well. For example, a hand over the heart expresses concern, while two arms folded over the chest sends a different message. To bring this into your students' awareness (and thus develop an important aspect of self), comment on your body language and theirs. Are they sitting slumped at their desks? What do they think about you sitting slumped at yours? How do they feel when you tap your foot waiting for their answers? What do they think clock watching conveys to you? Remind them that during any given class, the number of words they can speak is limited, yet the language of their bodies is not. You will receive many messages a day through their body language. What do they want theirs to be? How would they like their future bosses to read these subtle, and sometimes, blatant messages?

"Ninety percent of emotional communication is non-verbal" (Brooks, 2011, p. 12).

One effective approach came from a teacher in Brooklyn, NY. Her students would slump in their chairs and she'd say, "Okay class, pretend you're on a date with someone new and you're really interested in the person. Show me." With a few giggles (release of energy) they would all sit up and look focused. Then she would joke, "Thanks! For a second I thought you weren't interested."

Repeat What You Think You've Heard

Sometimes we subtly alter what is said (think of the game of Telephone mentioned above), which can lead to misinterpreting the problem or addressing the wrong issue. To make sure you are on point, try to repeat exactly what your student has said: "I hear you saying that math will never be important to you no matter how much I try to convince you. Is that right?" You may be surprised to find that you misinterpreted what was being expressed: "Not exactly. I said that math won't help me in my soccer career, so why bother?" Why waste time battling the wrong issue? Reflecting what you think is the issue clears up potential further miscommunication.

Social Skill 2: Cooperation

Cooperation is the foundation for collaboration, deemed a 21st century skill (although it has been around since the beginning of civilization!). However, cooperation can only flourish when the self feels safe and appreciated. A false self will not cooperate well, for fear of being seen—truly seen. Likewise, someone who is easily shamed will hide and choose a teamwork activity that is the least likely to draw attention. Such individuals will lose the opportunity to develop important skills, let alone work in a globally competitive marketplace. Cooperation is bolstered when the self is supported.

Sharing ideas and building upon them, dividing work and taking responsibility, and recognizing the strengths of others and utilizing them are abilities that all depend on trusted cooperation. As such, use more specific icebreakers that encourage group trust (such as catching one another from a backwards fall) and/or group contribution (such as each having to add a line to a song).

Intervention 6.2: Collaborating
From Small to Larger Groups

To focus on the need for cooperation, one teacher we know had each student write down the five traits he or she thought were most important for succeeding in life. After they were finished, they had to join into groups of three, share their traits, and agree upon the top five. Once a decision was made (they had a time limit), the groups joined one another to make groups of six, once again sharing their top five traits. The task then was for the groups of six to decide on the top five characteristics from the 10 brought to the group. Groups continued to join until the whole class came together and decided upon the final five characteristics. This exercise clearly demanded that the students reflect, cooperate, negotiate, and listen. As a clever way to tap into your classroom's collective consciousness, it is also an excellent exercise for coming up with all sorts of democratically chosen lists, such as classroom rules (which promotes morality), and even five traits of an effective teacher (imagine their list!).

Communication and cooperation promote the ability to get along with each other. Please work on these skills before moving on to the next step: teamwork.

TEAMWORK

Learning how to work in groups in a collaborative, nonjudgmental, and noncritical way is essential in today's globally competitive marketplace. Use your students' sociability to your advantage to develop team skills. Encourage group work whenever possible (Jacobs, 2011). Of course, you will not always be able to allow them to work with just their friends, but indeed, working with others with whom they do not normally hang out helps students manage their emotions and develop empathy, resilience, self-control, listening skills, and effective communication. As they work and connect with others, their sense of self is further developed and solidified.

Educator and speaker Heidi Hayes Jacobs reported middle school students' top three answers to how they would best like to learn: *in groups with friends,* doing practical things, and using computers. High school students' top choices are through discussion, debate, and *group projects* (Jacobs, 2011). Notice the social aspect of their choices. Students *want* to learn in a social way. In alignment with that desire, we want to strengthen the neuronal pathways for collaboration, communication, and cooperation to best prepare them for their futures.

When people work alone, they are free to allow their minds to wander. When in a small group, that same person is held accountable by the presence of her teammates. Spacing out is more difficult when your peers are expecting you to help them. As a result, when in a group, a student is also more likely to discover his self through the reflections of those around him. Group work also alters the decision-making process. As members share their opinions and thoughts, the group will need to decide which ideas are the best to move forward. This deliberation process demands engagement and self-reflection, strengthening the self-concept. These are all contributing factors as to why project-based learning is so effective and popular.

Often, however, teachers lament that "I tried having my students work in groups, but it's always a disaster." To make the most of teamwork, award-winning teacher Erin Filner from Fox Lane Middle School, Bedford, NY, points out that

> Teamwork involves a set of specific skills that need to be taught explicitly. It is a mistake to throw kids together and expect them to work cooperatively and effectively without being specifically taught the behaviors a teacher wants to see. If a teacher expects students to listen to each other, then what listening "looks like and sounds like" needs to be shown and demonstrated. This can be taught through a "T-chart" (for example a pro and con chart) and through role-play activities.

Filner goes on to explain that in a small group, for all kids to be invested, each team member must be assigned a specific—and relatively important—job. It must be clear that each job is necessary for group success. In her class, each group must have an Activity Director (group facilitator), Task Master (responsible for keeping the group members "on task" and focused), a Materials Collector, a Time Keeper, and a Reporter. While in reality some tasks require more leadership and responsibility than others, all jobs are necessary for complete group success.

In addition, Filner says, "Prior to creating teams/cooperative groups, it is essential to teach the value of different learning styles so that the premise of joining together is that we all have strengths and none of us is 'perfect' by ourselves." Indeed, teamwork does underscore the meaning of being a group member and a student's overall responsibility to the group. Eighth-grade physics teacher Charles Duveen highlights the beneficial life skills that teamwork provides when a team member falls ill. He writes,

In business, "the show must go on." This means that even when someone is a key person, no one is irreplaceable. This means that you must develop as a good team, a team will make up for anyone who is unable to attend. When the lead pitcher pulls out his arm, do the Yankees ask to postpone the game? Nope. They just get a replacement. I always look forward to having someone absent, especially one of the managers. It tests the resiliency of the whole team. Everybody does the best they can. I'll never forget the time we had an illness going through the school, and the Final Design Review was underway at the Stamford Hilton Hotel. One class got hit with four—that's right FOUR—teammates that were too sick to go. The team members not only stood in for the missing presenters, they went on to take first place in the competition—a real demonstration of teamwork. And if I remember correctly, one of the missing didn't even let anyone know they weren't showing up—how bad is that? (Charles Duveen, Applied Physics Teacher, Rippowam Cisqua School, Bedford, NY)

Leadership Is Not for Everyone

Leadership skills have been touted as desirable for all, but the truth is, not everyone is meant to be a leader. And that's okay! When students learn who they are in relation to group work (not necessarily being the leader), they learn what skills they bring to help reach the group's end goal. Have students brainstorm—with your guidance, of course—different group roles and the character traits that may be relevant to each. Recognizing how they best contribute and how they can accommodate the group needs on a team project is a skill they will need and employ forever.

Having students collaborate toward an end goal with people whom they may not know or like is a critical life skill that students will forever employ. Therefore, knowing who *they* are and how they best contribute when working in groups is invaluable and can make the difference between keeping a job or losing one. Thus, employ group work when possible and appropriate and ask students questions about the process. Below is a list of questions. Consider sharing the list with students before they work in groups so they are more cognizant of what they will have to answer after.

- *What made you more comfortable as you tackled the project: being a leader or being a follower?*

- *How were disagreements handled? Describe one. What were the issues? Explain both sides.*
- *Did you use your imagination?*
- *How did you come to your decisions? Who was the most vocal? The least?*
- *Name one creative idea you offered. Name a creative idea someone else offered.*
- *What would you have changed?*
- *What did you learn about yourself in the process?*

Remember, emotions are bound to evolve when two or more people work together. However, if the emotion is negative, information will be sent to the reactive centers of the brain, students may become defensive, and cognition will shut down. Teaching self skills enables students to manage emotions in order to work cooperatively, resulting in more effective education (Combs, 1991).

The Benefits of Working in Groups:

- Promotes self-reflection
- Develops group member identity as to role and purpose
- Encourages taking another person's point of view—empathy and compassion
- Promotes responsibility
- Provides practice for effective communication
- Makes meaningful connections happen
- They like you for letting them talk with their friends during class. (Jacobs, 2011; Yalom, 1995)

Consolidate information via group activities, as students often prefer and acquire new information better when presented in smaller doses. To capitalize on this, have students form small groups to discuss your lessons. Done strategically and with the previous skills set in place (communication and cooperation), students take their learning to the next level.

Because learning is such an emotional process, when students are forced to work in groups with people with whom they do not get along or by whom they feel threatened, less learning takes place. Until we teach how to get along with people, we are not providing students with *life* skills. The bottom line is, don't throw students together who don't have the first skill sets in place (communication, cooperation) and who can't get along with each other. Learning won't take place and frustration levels will rise. Instead, take the necessary time to teach the skills required to work together. In the end, it will prove to be more valuable than the lesson of the day since it is something they are guaranteed to take with them for life.

Intervention 6.3: Rotations

Every 20 minutes or so have students break into small groups and discuss what you've just taught them. Preassign groups and rotate the groups each week or so. Have students try different roles in the group (leader, note taker, presenter of ideas). Provide a prompt for them to discuss and present their thoughts. For instance, if you spoke about brain functions, you may choose the prompt: *Each person summarize the function of a different brain structure and together discuss the importance of each.* Groups can present their thoughts or write them down for collection at the end of class. This is a wonderful precursor to project-based learning skills.

Handling Conflicts in Groups

Lest we forget, the classroom in and of itself is a group setting. Hence, it affords many chances to model leadership, to listen, to resolve conflicts, and to balance the needs of each group member (student) so that the task at hand is accomplished (learning). Below are a few ideas for handling those conflicts and juggling the disparate needs of your students. (If you've never had a conflict in your classroom, feel free to skip to the end.)

Conflicts are bound to emerge. Sadly, however, student conflict is one of the top reasons why teachers burn out. The whole idea of teaching to the self is a proactive strategy to mitigate conflict. As you bring forth the self, a sense of pride and motivation is born. Conflict can either retard or actually strengthen that potential growth. To model appropriate behavior and, of course, to support each student's sense of self in your classroom climate, we offer the following techniques in case you encounter inclement weather:

Quickly!

Deal with conflicts right away whenever possible (besides benefiting your classroom, it benefits your students' brains—you don't want those synapses laying down tracks of negativity). Students often need help immediately identifying what led to the conflict as well as how to solve it.

If emotions have gotten out of hand, allow for a "cooling off" period first, if necessary. However, do return to the issue and make sure it is discussed and resolved. Unresolved issues fester in your classroom, causing disconnect and resistance. Students may also continue to repeat this unhealthy pattern of "sweeping things under the carpet." Your students are served well when they learn that respectful communication about an issue is most effective in dealing with conflict.

Keep Your Sense of Humor

Do your students find you to be too serious? The students we have worked with generally feel that adults are "too serious." After watching many interactions between students and teachers over the years, we can understand this perspective. Adults are primarily the ones enforcing rules, setting limits, and following agendas. Students' favorite teachers are largely those who smile and laugh with them—actions that promote connection and dispense dopamine while still maintaining structure, safety, and balance.

Thus, if faced with a potentially difficult situation, consider taking a proactive, positive, more light-hearted approach: "The rocket launcher is for science class, yet here it is in the cafeteria with a bowl of pasta on it primed for liftoff. That's remarkable! But, we do need it for science . . . , so before we start putting consequences on removing the rocket launcher from the science lab, who would like to return it to its rightful place for me?" You are sure to get a few volunteers. This way, the subject is the rocket launcher, not the student. As such, the student responsible for moving the rocket launcher is less likely to become defensive. Once she is identified, consider talking privately to her about her actions rather than in front of her friends. Private reprimands decrease embarrassment and thus respect the self.

Teacher Illustration 6.4: Humor in Learning

Victor Manielly, Education Specialist, Durham, NC

Six months into teaching English in China and with the beginning of a new semester, I inherited a class from a teacher who moved to another city. I could tell from the first 5 minutes that Michelle was going to be a tough nut to crack. She didn't smile at all the first day. This is incredibly rare here. Chinese students are, for the most part, super happy and uber-motivated. Michelle decided she wanted to be the exception with some serious power frowning. This was instantly a challenge to which I dedicated myself.

In my first class, I took pictures of the kids and cropped them to get "head shots." We were studying animals for the unit, so in Week 2, after introducing pictures of the animals, the heads of students would pop up on the power points in place of the animal's head. The laughter caused a delicious din. Michelle's head popped up on the top of a giraffe. For the briefest of moments, her frown was cracked. In that moment, I knew progress was and would be made.

Use Others to Bring the Class Back to Task

Students can't focus until you have dealt with distractions. But for every student trying to escape your learning path, many exist who are firmly standing on it. Positive peer pressure can be used as an incentive for those who seek to "take a left" from learning. Enlist the help of those who want to learn by bridging their desires with students who are disrupting the class. The example below illustrates how students can help each other ease the tension while promoting connections and compassion.

Intervention 6.4: Bridging

When one or two students attempt to divert your learning path, and when tension is *not high*, try bringing another student or two into the action through an intervention called bridging. You may ask, "Jose, how do you understand this problem between Craig and Ibby?" Jose may be able to enlighten you, and them, by offering his feelings about the situation.

For example, Jose may have his own feelings about the situation between Ibby and Craig and may remark that whatever is going on needs to be handled fast because it's bothering him. When Ibby and Craig hear that their situation is troubling to others, they may settle things, or you may "bridge" for another person to enter the dialogue: "Alise, do you have any suggestions on how we can help Ibby and Craig resolve this so that we can get back to the task of learning, which Jose, for one, would really appreciate?" Now Alise may have a few helpful suggestions. These suggestions coming from a peer, rather than an adult, may feel less threatening to Ibby and Craig. They may be more motivated to resolve their issues when faced with the understanding that their peers are affected by their actions. Alise and Jose feel their self and learning potentials were respected. The latent message is that *learning comes first, but if you can't join us, I'm not going to shame you; I'm going to help you get back on track.*

However, be sure to choose your more emotionally aware and compassionate students the first few times you do this so that they hopefully will emulate to the class how to conduct themselves. Choosing someone with a history of shame will only push those shame buttons and likely cause him or her to withdraw from the classroom rather than connect. (The time you take away from your demanding schedule to address distractions in this manner will be about 5 minutes and will curtail future distractions from taking away more time.)

Larger and more imbedded conflicts (especially those that cause increased levels of tension) are ultimately the responsibility of the school (teachers, counselors, coaches, etc.), not the students. Teachers, after all, are the ones in the room with the experience, maturity, wisdom, insight, and calm patience to manage the classroom. As the lone person in the midst of flying emotional debris, your climate control comes in the form of social and emotional resonance with your students. You cannot instantaneously acquire resonance in a storm—it needs to be built each and every day in the moment to moment of teaching and connecting with your students. The more connected you are to your students, the more control you will have when a storm hits. When you have made daily connections, you can be the calm in the storm that helps your students to feel safe.

CHAPTER SUMMARY

Check In With Your Self

When you were in middle school and high school, what was your focus? Was it academics? Your family life? Your social life? How do you regard the social world of your students—a hindrance or a tool for learning?

Interventions

Telephone

Collaborate from small to larger groups

Rotations

Bridging

(Also keep in mind the concepts of icebreakers, classroom set up, setting rules, modeling behavior, being approachable, your tone of voice, making eye contact, using names, keeping a sense of humor.)

Activity: Address Social Concerns

Situation	Goal	Intervention
Describe a situation you hope to improve. *I have two couples in my class who can't stop staring at each other and distracting the other students.*	What do you hope to achieve with the student? *Bring all the students, especially the stargazing couples, back to earth to listen and learn.*	Which intervention in the chapter will you use? *Bridging*

Outcome
List the time frame and overall impressions. *When the stargazing couples moved to whispering loudly, I asked Joselyn if the whispering bothered her. I misjudged Joselyn—she just shook her head no. But then Trevor spoke up and said, "It's annoying to me. I mean, get a room why don't you." I thought it might get ugly for a moment, but when giggles ensued, I opened up the discussion to everyone in the classroom. We talked about PDA and what was okay and what was not . . . it was a very lively discussion, and although I didn't quite get through the whole lesson plan, stargazers were definitely less disruptive in the following days.*

Now construct a chart from your experience.

The Physical Self: Support the Physical Self for Optimal Overall Health

Those who think they have not the time for bodily exercise will sooner or later have to find time for illness.

—Edward Stanley

WHAT YOU WILL LEARN IN THIS CHAPTER

This chapter covers Step 6: Support the physical self for optimal overall health. In this chapter, you will learn

- How exercise impacts overall health
- How nutrition impacts overall health
- How sleep impacts overall health
- How the mind and body are intrinsically connected
- How the physical self can be supported in the classroom

THE IMPORTANCE OF PHYSICAL HEALTH

When physically healthy, the ability to focus on the important tasks at hand—academics, building our identities, managing emotions, forming meaningful relationships—becomes far easier. But when we don't eat well, exercise, or get enough sleep, we simply can't function optimally and our performance suffers accordingly.

Bogged down with mandates, schools are cutting important health-related activities and lessons. This need not be the case, especially since health is arguably the most important subject from which every single student benefits for his or her entire life. This chapter will include suggested interventions to weave the physical self into curriculum and daily activities.

EXERCISE AND HEALTH

Exercise is the key ingredient to a healthy lifestyle. It has been cited as an antidote to nearly every ailment, including heart disease, diabetes, cancer, high blood pressure, high cholesterol, and weak bones, to name just a few. Researchers have also found a link between exercise and cognitive improvement (Reynolds, 2012). Indeed, according to Martin Seligman, poor physical fitness puts you more at risk for death in general, and especially for cardiovascular-related disease (Seligman, 2011). Moreover, his conclusions point to the very real possibility that the real epidemic in this country may not be obesity per se, but inactivity. Seligman calculates that "the fit—but fat—individual has almost half the risk of death as the unfit, fat individual" (p. 217). The more physically active a person is, the less at risk for death—across the board.

Of course, the habits your students create *now* will determine the health risk factors they face later. Moreover, research has found that "children who are physically active and fit tend to perform better in the classroom," have better attendance, fewer disciplinary problems including involvement in drugs, alcohol, violence, or truancy (www.ActiveLivingResearch.org). Further research also indicates that many students' individual passions lie in the sports arena. When such passions are supported, those students are generally less depressed, less worried, more resilient, more satisfied with life overall, and perform better in school (www.Search-Institute.org). The benefits of a strong physical fitness program are far-reaching and can no longer be delegated to a second tier status in education.

However, many students today are just not interested in physical activity. This generation lives among a fast-paced, want-it-now, immediate gratification, quick-fix mentality preferring to take their exercise in pill form and wash it down with a diet coke. Indeed, factors such as the increase in video games, number of TV channels, and even public transport have created a culture in which activity is undervalued, or at least, underpracticed. Therefore, merely teaching the importance of daily exercise is not resonating with many. Those messages need to be coupled with positive experiences that resonate with students' sense of selves.

Spur the Body: What Do Students Want to Do?

Many of the students with whom we spoke told us that the sports programs or gym classes were boring, that teachers needed to come up with creative, innovative ways to do sports. Are we trying to impose our idea of athleticism on them and failing? Why not find out what they would like? What form of exercise does your population prefer? Moreover, what might your students' experience be if they simply spent a class walking through the woods? Climbing stairs through the school? Rearranging the storage room? These are all physical activities that bring health benefits (even though students might not see them in such a manner). Understanding that physical health can be achieved through regular activities rather than organized sports can bring greater awareness about their choices and their health.

Programs work well when they are varied, reach a broad range of students, and are innovative to connect with the modern world of today's youth. Add unexpected twists to more traditional games to keep the sport fresh. For example, you might try reversing the direction of the bases in baseball or have half the indoor kickball team wear blinders so teammates need to coach them through the bases (building teamwork skills, communication, and empathy). Tai Chi, dance (various forms), kickboxing, rock climbing, and even unusual obstacle courses can create excitement and inspiration in your students. Less traditional or popular physical activities are beneficial, as they broaden the options for student activity.

Intervention 7.1: Community Resources: Variety at a Limited Cost

Schools have varying degrees of funding for sports programs. Whether you can bring in a rock wall for a week, a circus for a day, or call the local gym and ask for a trainer for a week—depends on your budget and protocol. Often community members are happy to offer their services. See what options exist in your neighborhood. Perhaps a few community members can teach a new exercise—students may engage more when the ideas feel fresh and new. Bringing in members of the community to help teach also adds to the sense of community and supports local business. Students learn not only what activities are available to them outside school, but also who is available to offer support. (Note: We realize many schools may have restrictions on this, so we apologize if you are unable to achieve this as we suggest it.)

Intervention 7.2: School Teams

Create teams within your grades or schoolwide to engage in some friendly physical competition. When students take the stairs or choose clever ways to exercise during an appropriate allotted time during the day (before school, after school, lunchtime, recess), they earn points for their team. Points are tallied over the course of the semester and/or year with the "winner" (in quotes because everyone wins when exercise is increased) receiving a school party, special meal from a local establishment, or even a discount at the school store.

In order to truly effect change, create awareness of the benefits not just by listing them, but by asking students to reflect upon them. How do they feel before gym class? After recess? Between class breaks? Have them keep track. Allow them to see that movement can often hit the "refresh" button for them.

Spur the Brain: Increase Movement

When students engage in play and laughter, they release dopamine and endorphins—chemicals associated with making connections with others and within our brains. When students sit all day (and they sit for thousands of hours by the time they graduate), they are often engaging the left, linear, analytical, logical side of their brain. This is patterned, repetitive, and can often feel like an engine in need of grease. Exercise provides the momentum to grease the wheels of cognitive capacity and gets students into the right side of their brains.

Intervention 7.3: Activity Breaks

If you don't have time for a full on recess, try activity breaks of just 5 to 10 minutes where you organize a short game of catch, calisthenics, or even a desk "crawl" where students need to weave in and out of desks quickly. This allows increased oxygen to reach the brain, improving concentration, and helping students to get back on academic track.

Keep a bag of balls handy in the classroom and try this: After a lesson, toss a few balls into the room, and have your students play catch in small groups. The assignment: With each ball toss have them name a topic discussed in the lesson (Willis, 2011a).

In Summary

Whatever we consider to be our personal exercise regime (or lack of) is very much a part of our identity. How fit we are tells the world how much we value health and exercise. A mindset that thinks, *I respect and work my body to keep it healthy*, will acquire a far different fitness level from a person who values sitting on the couch all day and never partakes in any form of exercise. *How* do we create the correct mindset? By making exercise part of the school atmosphere, by incorporating programs that resonate with them, not only with us, and by demonstrating that being fit is an important element to a healthy life. By incorporating the interventions discussed thus far, your students' physical selves will not only be called to the present in the classroom, but will also be more thoroughly integrated into their overall identity.

> **Check In With Your Self**
>
> Do you believe exercise facilitates learning? What are you doing to incorporate a program or lesson plan that includes an awareness of the physical self?

NUTRITION AND HEALTH

Two-thirds of Americans are overweight or obese (Brody, 2012), causing significant health problems at a young age and escalating later in life. Habits develop early in life—in the brain we make those neuronal connections during the teen years or we prune them—setting us up for a healthy lifestyle or sedentary disaster. This is why creating healthy eating habits now and encouraging a "fit" mentality will develop a mindset full of beneficial habits and patterns—for life.

The numbers change almost weekly, but the most recent finding as we write this indicate that 17% of children aged 2 to 19 are obese, close to three times the rate in 1980. In addition, Type II diabetes, a preventable disease, is on the rise. Historically, children rarely got Type II, but today, thousands of children are struggling with it nationwide, with over 2 million more already at risk. Once someone is diagnosed with Type II diabetes, the chances of reversing it are slim, leaving many children at an increased risk for heart disease and cardiovascular complications for life (www.diabetes.org).

With a sedentary lifestyle (addressed above) and with sugary ads that bombard them constantly, many children now expect the sweet, uncomplicated access to junk food (both of the snack and mealtime variety, i.e., sugary cereal, chocolate milk, sweetened applesauce). Thus, the challenge we face in informing and changing our children's habits is formidable, but certainly not insurmountable. Most schools teach nutrition. However, teaching students about MyPlate is only a very small step toward effecting change and lifelong habits. A program that merely teaches that whole grains are a better choice than white flour products won't make an impression (and effect change) as readily as a program that focuses on *the self in relation to nutrition*. Creating personally meaningful assignments around healthy eating and smart food choices is therefore essential in helping students relate to the material. Is the nutrition information in your school provided in a manner that registers with your students' desire to grow and reach their potentials?

Intervention 7.4: Nutrition Assignment

Have your students conduct a "longitudinal study" of their eating habits. Divide the class into three or more groups/teams. Have each team conduct a nutritional investigation and subsequent experiment. The investigation involves each team choosing a different category from the following list: Interview local registered nutritionists, prepare shopping lists (compare prices of nutritionally potent food costs versus poor-choice food costs), talk to the local food purveyors, research local sustainable food sources. (Your list may vary.) Once they have investigated a certain avenue of nutrition, then they conduct the experiment: Have them adjust their own nutritional choices according to the information they gathered, and keep track of the changes made over the course of a week. Students can use graphing, charting, illustrations, storyboards, or other devices of their choosing. These changes and/or comparisons may include caloric considerations, nutritional quality, sustainable sources, environmental concerns, or whatever information they gleaned from their investigations.

Once the students understand the significance of a healthy diet and how that plays out in the form of calories, nutrition, and energy sources, they must make a prediction on the changes they will be able to incorporate in their own lives by the end of the following week. For instance, Stella has worked on caloric changes she learned by reading labels at the supermarket. She charts that in 1 week she has dropped her caloric intake by 185 calories (and the group dropped by 375). She predicts that if she can continue on this path, she will feel less sluggish, have more focus, maybe even lose some weight, and overall, feel healthier. The point of the prediction is to help students involve their self in their learning. When the self is involved, change is more likely.

Teacher Illustration 7.4: Nutrition Assignment

Amanda Gerber, Health Educator, Bedford Central School District, Bedford, NY

During the nutrition mini unit with my sixth graders, we talk about healthy snacking. I make sure no one in the class has an allergy, and then I bring in all the materials for the students to make their own smoothies. This way they have the opportunity to not just talk about what's healthy, but to actually eat it! This gives some of

Check In With Your Self

Think about how you felt the last time you were sleep deprived. Were you eager to face the day or did you feel less than optimal? Did you feel your self was at its best or compromised?

them an opportunity to try fruits they haven't before, and some of them are surprised by how tasty smoothies can be. They are also easy to make, which is key as well. The students love the activity because they take a break from the normal lecture format and work together doing something extremely beneficial for them.

SLEEP AND HEALTH

Many teens suffer from treatable sleep disorders, such as narcolepsy, insomnia, restless legs syndrome, or sleep apnea. (National Sleep Foundation, 2012)

Our self-concept is extremely wrapped up in our sleep.

A student ready to learn.

A student not prepared for learning.

Teens and Sleep

Most teens do not get their recommended hours of sleep. For many, this results in sleep deprivation. Sleep deprivation affects their concentration, memory, focus, mood, immune system, coordination, decisions, and overall health. A lack of sleep can also increase the risk for accidents, obesity (sleep deprivation causes an increase in appetite), mental health issues, and other physical health concerns. According to the National Sleep Foundation, teens (10 to 17 years old) need 8.5 to 9.25 hours of sleep, while adults need 7 to 9 hours. (Yes, sleep needs are individual, but in general, certain age groups need a set amount.) Unfortunately, with mounting academic pressures, extracurricular activities, and an enthusiastic social life, this amount of sleep escapes most teens. In fact, 62% of high school students get insufficient sleep.

Part of the reason for this has to do with the current normative start times that are at odds with a teenager's natural sleep cycle. As teens reach puberty, their endocrine system shifts the production time of melatonin, the brain chemical responsible for sleepiness. It is secreted from about 11 p.m. until 8 a.m.—resulting in most teenagers' desire to stay up later and sleep longer. However, the current start time of most high schools asks teens to rise well before their melatonin cycle is complete, causing them to be groggy during morning classes. They are literally fighting their biological clock to stay awake. The disruption of the sleep cycle can result in secondary symptoms such as depression, frustration, and alcohol and drug use.

Moreover, the teen brain is still developing. As discussed in Chapter 5, the regions associated with planning ahead and impulse control are located in the prefrontal cortex, which is not fully formed until the mid-twenties. Thus, their ability to plan ahead for tests (instead of cramming) and to manage their time well is already compromised. A lack of sleep will only compound the situation as sleep helps this part of the brain establish itself. Thus, at no other time is establishing regular and steady sleep patterns more important, and yet at no other time is sleep more disrupted for the average American teen.

Research from two separate Minnesota school districts reveal promising benefits when high schools switch their start times to accommodate teen sleep cycles. When these school districts delayed their start time, data showed that drop out and depression rates decreased while students reported higher grades. Meanwhile, the typical initial concerns from parents about the later start time (logistics with younger children, later after-school activities, and transportation) appear to be unfounded. After the first year, 92% of parents reported that they preferred the later start times (University of Minnesota, 2012).

Incorporate the Self

But again, just as with nutrition and exercise, teaching students about the importance of a good night's sleep may go in one ear and out the other without a personal motivator or context in which they can place the information. A simple Q&A to assess their sleep habits, schedules, and belief systems enables self-reflection and perhaps even motivation to seek change.

Intervention 7.5: Time Management

Teach time management using visual cues to help teens see that sleep is a vital part of their functioning self. Have students keep track of how they spend their time each day and then, at the end of the week, have them fill in a pie chart based on their accumulated research. The chart will include daily hours spent: eating, sleeping, at school, exercising, socializing, playing with an electronic device, with family, homework, working a job, and other activities. When students see how they spend their time and the number of hours they sleep each night compared to the recommended level, the information may resonate more with them because it has become more personal. To consolidate the information, have them work in groups, collaborating on ideas and strategies for planning ahead and allocating time. Have the groups meet as one to discuss all the ideas discovered.

Healthful Sleep Habits

The following are general guidelines for better sleep habits. Please share them and discuss them with your students.

- Establish regular sleep and wake times, even on the weekends. (Teens rarely abide by this, as weekends are their time to "catch up," but it is something to reach toward.)
- Create routines before bed: What are your students' bedtime rituals? Shower, brush teeth, wash face, set clothes out for the next day, set alarm, and then listen to music? Whatever the process surrounding going to sleep, they should try to make elements repetitive, like an ingrained habit. This "teaches" the body that sleep is on its way. The following information may be surprising, but reading before bed is not recommended. (Gasp! Don't we encourage this and even do it ourselves?) Apparently, doing anything in bed (other than sleep and sex) is not recommended if you choose to keep your bedroom free from distractions that may curtail sleep efforts. If kids

equate reading with sleep, how might that fare in your classroom when they are asked to read eight pages of Shakespeare?

- Create a comfortable sleep environment: Check that the temperature is set at the right level for you, the blinds are shut, and enough blankets are on the bed.
- Turn off the television, computer, and the iPad: Light-emitting screens inhibit quality of sleep (Milian, 2010). The content stimulates the brain and the bright screen inhibits serotonin secretion. However, with teens being so reliant on electronic devices, this suggestion may be met with much resistance. As such, suggest shortening the length of time they use those devices right before bed.
- Turn off the cell phone: Many teens sleep with their cell phones on and at hand (often hiding them under their pillows). Many are awakened during the night to engage in conversations, sometimes without remembering them the next morning. Again, even the light from this screen will significantly disrupt their sleep cycles (Horstman, 2009).
- Try to avoid naps: If teens do want to nap, suggest napping before 3 p.m. and for no more than 20 minutes. Otherwise, teens are likely to find themselves up at night.
- Eat earlier in the evening so you have a chance to digest: Sleepfoundation.org suggests that you do not eat 2 to 3 hours before bedtime, and many nutritionists will recommend that you watch what you eat at night. Sugary and fatty snacks are not good for digestion or sleep.
- Exercise during the day. (See? Something else it benefits!)
- Avoid caffeine after 4 p.m. (and chocolate has caffeine).
- Incorporate foods that promote sleep. The following five foods aid in sleep as long as they are eaten an hour or two before intended lights out: grapes, warm milk, peanuts, cottage cheese, and oatmeal (Clark, 2012).

Intervention 7.6: Create Healthful Habits

To help students establish better sleep habits, show them first that you respect the necessity of sleep: Try not to arrive in class sleep deprived yourself. Also, honor their ability to only complete so much homework per night. Discuss with your fellow teachers large projects and their due dates (for example, assign a day of the week that each subject area is granted as their test day) so that multiple projects are not all scheduled to be completed the same day. Let students know that you have considered their overall homework load when creating their homework assignments. By acknowledging that you are being cognizant of their need to balance work, family, friends, and sleep, you send the clear message that all such areas are important. In addition, have them write down their current sleep patterns and routines and then compare them with the guidelines above.

THE MIND/BODY CONNECTION

Your body and mind are intrinsically connected. In fact, in other cultures mind and body are not separated; only Western medicine makes this distinction. Understanding this connection allows us to capitalize on its powers and to fully integrate the physical self into our overall identity. In the not so distant past, the mind/body connection has been diminished as something that was nice in theory but not supported by scientific research. Yet today, thousands of research studies support not only its authenticity but underscore its immense power.

The Science Behind the Connection

You are now familiar with neurons (nerve cells) in the brain (Chapter 5), but did you know that neurons are in the body as well? Neurons transmit important mind/body information. Molecules found throughout the body send signals to one another in response to an experience or situation, releasing appropriate chemical reactions based on our emotional response to the experience or situation. Candace Pert, PhD, calls these "molecules of emotion." In her book, *Everything You Need to Know to Feel Go(o)d* (2006), she writes, "your symptoms are in your body, but they are also always in your mind, whether consciously or subconsciously. Mind and body are not split in two, so what happens in one occurs in the other, too" (p. 35).

A fascinating mind/body example is found in people who have MPD (Multiple Personality Disorder). Often, if one personality has an allergy, scar, or physical issue, it goes away when another personality becomes dominant. Even medical conditions possessed by one personality will disappear with another personality. Dr. Bennett Braun of the International Society for the Study of Multiple Personality in Chicago has documented a case in which all of a patient's personalities were allergic to orange juice, except one. If an allergic personality drank the juice, he would break into a rash. But, when the patient switched to a personality that was not allergic to orange juice, the rash would disappear and orange juice did not cause an issue (Talbot, 1991).

Ways to Bring Forth the Mind/Body Awareness

The idea of using the mind to heal the body has been around for centuries. Below are a few examples of how the mind can help us heal and how you can pass along this information to your students. In this way, you can help them realize the power of their minds and put that power to work in whatever capacity your students deem best suited for them, ultimately supporting both the physical and whole self.

Visualization: Does It Really Work?

Visualization can enhance performance almost as well as actual practice. Dr. Judd Blaslotto from the University of Chicago studied free-throw basketball shots among three groups of people. The base-line free-throw success rate was first established, and the participants were then randomly allocated to a group with specific instructions for 30 days. The results were as follows:

Group 3 did not practice or visualize their free-throws and showed no improvement.

Group 1 practiced free-throws for an hour a day. They improved their performance by 24%.

Group 2 merely visualized shooting free-throws, without stepping foot on a basketball court. They improved their free-throws by 23%! (Haefner, 2012)

Other experiments have replicated this approach with similar findings (Clark, 1960). But make no mistake. You cannot attain a cardio workout while sitting on the couch imagining running a marathon. Some things we must actually do to reap the rewards. However, visualization does allow us to harness the power of our minds for improving our selves.

Almost all professional athletes use some type of visualization to improve their abilities. Many students idolize sports stars. Have your students research what their favorite athletes do to improve their performance.

Intervention 7.7: Visualization

Conduct an experiment of your own. Have students replicate Dr. Blaslotto's research using basketball, penalty kicks, ping pong accuracy, or any number of clever skill sets your students choose. Have them work in teams, create charts, graph progress, and make predictions. As they experience the process, they will become motivated to visualize all sorts of success!

Mindfulness

Mindfulness is the act of *bringing awareness to the present moment* without judgment. It challenges our tendency to lament over the past or worry about the future while encouraging awareness, acceptance, and compassion. By being present in the here and now, the practitioner reaps many benefits: increased immune function, increase concentration, decreased stress, decreased recurrence of depression, and increased resilience (Firestone, 2013).

Mindfulness builds self-awareness, which helps in emotional regulation (the focus of Chapters 3 and 4). This is why many mental health professionals teach their clients to use mindfulness: It helps them monitor their thoughts and feelings and thereby control impulses. Your students can reap the same benefits.

Intervention 7.8: Mindfulness Exercise

Explain to your students what mindfulness is and why you think it will help them. Then suggest a 5-minute exercise for them to try at home. Have students choose a time (mealtime, sitting in nature, watching a sport, bedtime) to close their eyes and experience for 1 minute all that is happening in that moment. Describe how in compelling, suspenseful, well-written books, the author often spends several paragraphs describing a scene: the mood, smells, sounds, energy, surroundings, the weather, people, personalities, etc. Have your students write their scenes as though they were that compelling author. You may have them turn in the written assignment or have a group discussion on what it was like to do the assignment. What does being present feel like? Is it difficult to achieve? Did they tend to pass judgment on themselves? What did they learn?

Teacher Illustration 7.8: Using Mindfulness to Manage Emotions

Elizabeth Messinger, Teacher of Humanities, Writing, and French, Rippowam Cisqua School, Bedford, NY

Part of the course description for the Allied Arts elective I teach reads: *Practicing mindfulness gives us the power to recognize what we're feeling so that we learn to control our responses, even in stressful situations.* One day, two girls, Jamie and Sandra, told me how their practice had paid off in this manner. In the process of collaborating on a science project, two of the peers they'd been partnered with had presented Jamie and Sandra with their assigned duties, as if it were already a done deal. "I was about to start telling them off," said Sandra, "but then Jamie and I caught each other's eye, and it was like we both just immediately recognized what was beginning to happen."

Anger had been the subject in mindfulness class that day. The class had learned the importance of stopping themselves from speaking or taking meaningful action any time they are in a feeling state that tends to be counterproductive to making good decisions. Doing so allows us to feel our emotions without being sabotaged by them. This rescued Sandra in the confrontation later: "I named the feeling inside, and that alone helped me to stop for a second, just like we'd learned in class." She then remembered a mantra I had taught them and managed to blurt out, "I'd like some time to think about that, then I'll get back to you." This allowed the time and space needed to calm the emotion and eventually work on an agreement.

Learning these practices early in life equips teens especially with a sound basis for the autonomy they crave at that age. Rather than letting their limbic core run riot, mindfulness helps them get a grip on their emotions by stationing awareness at the helm of their lives, and thereby providing the possibility of making more reasoned and reasonable decisions.

Meditation

Meditation, a form of mindfulness, seeks to quiet the mind as well, but the focus is inward on a specific thought rather than being more attuned to the outside moment. In Chapter 5, meditation is discussed as a way to relieve stress and boost cognitive functions. Here, we would like to emphasize meditation's mind/body benefits: A recent study revealed the ability of meditation to reduce the risk of heart attacks and strokes as well as lower blood pressure and relieve anger. Study author Robert Schneider concludes, "What this is saying is that mind/body interventions can have an effect [on health] as big as conventional medications" ("Meditation's Health Benefits," 2012).

Meditation in schools is growing in practice. Several research studies have shown that students benefit greatly through in-school meditation. Those benefits include (but are not limited to): decreased anxiety, decreased test anxiety, decreased truancy, decreased suspensions, improved attention, improved social skills, and improved self-regulation (Vega, 2012).

Notice that many of these benefits involve self skills. Meditation increases the presence and confidence of the self.

Intervention 7.9: Meditation

Try meditation in your classroom. Introduce it. Explain the benefits and allow students to discover for themselves how it fits into their worlds. You could even make it a homework assignment: Meditate for 10 minutes this afternoon and write about the process. Of course you will need to provide instruction. Have students sit comfortably and quietly and close their eyes. Ask them to focus on their breathing and to simply observe the thoughts that enter their minds. They may notice feelings or thoughts, but the goal is simply to allow them to occur without judgment while seeking to maintain their focus on their breathing. Remind students that some practitioners have spent months and months to achieve the desired state. Meditation is not easy for some—the mind's will to produce thoughts and judgments is strong, especially in the teen mind! So patience, forgiveness, and the right mental fortitude help.

Teacher Illustration 7.9: Decrease Competition and Increase Self-Awareness

Greville Henwood, Owner and Founder of GroovyKids Yoga in Los Angeles, CA

While working with the son of a successful film and TV producer, I kept coming up against a proverbial brick wall. He accepted me as a teacher/mentor, and more important, himself as a student, only when I managed to convince him that there is no competition in yoga or meditation and that you cannot be good or bad at something that is nonquantifiable. He didn't have to be the expert, nor was he required to be the finished article, but only to be treading a path. This caused a seismic shift in him and his stress level. His general demeanor and attitude changed dramatically. This 17-year-old only child who was angry at the world and everyone in it, suddenly dropped his defenses with me. As a result he passed his exams easily and went on to Boston University, where he graduated and is now a successful film and TV producer in his own right, who, coincidentally, works closely with his dad and stopped seeing his parents as enemies.

To this day, we all remain fast friends, and the family often refers to me as their adopted son. The lad in question refers to me as his brother from another mother.

And all because I got him to see that yoga and meditation are process oriented, not result driven.

THE PHYSICAL SELF IN THE CLASSROOM

In Sir Ken Robinson's book, *The Element* (2009), he writes about the world-renowned dancer and choreographer Gillian Lynn. When Gillian was a little girl, she appeared energetic in class, unable to concentrate or focus. Her mother brought her to a doctor. The three spoke for a while, and then the doctor and the mother left the room, but not before the doctor flipped on the radio. When the doctor and mother observed Gillian from outside, she was dancing. The doctor turned to the mother and said Gillian did not need a doctor. What she needed was dance lessons. While reflecting on this time in her life, Gillian remarked, "'I walked into this room, and it was full of people like me. People who couldn't sit still. People who had to move to think'" (p. 3). Gillian eventually joined the Royal Ballet Company in London and worked with Andrew Lloyd Weber on many Broadway sensations. Robinson writes, "Gillian wasn't a problem child. She didn't need to go away to a special school. She just needed to be who she really was" (p. 4).

Some children are not born to sit still. For about 50% of your student population, sitting still is most likely *not* a natural state. Lest we forget, teenage boys have huge amounts of hormones flowing through their bodies: What you see out on the sports field is an extension of the natural inclination for boys to be more physical (yes, we are generalizing). Asking them to sit still for long hours on end can be very difficult. Moreover, some evidence exists that boys process better when moving (Villano, 2011), and as studies in neuroscience and exercise tell us, movement is good for all brain functions, including memory and comprehension (Brody, 2012).

Asking students to "sit still" decreases their focus—they now need to concentrate on sitting still (or not tapping their pencil, or twirling their hair) rather than your teaching. Thus, you may wish to allow students to get up and move around if need be. Let your students know that standing or pacing in the back of the classroom where they are less likely to distract other students is acceptable. (It will certainly be less distracting than some of the disruptions they will cause otherwise.) You may even suggest a quick "water fountain" break for those who often seem bursting at the seams (discussed beforehand with individuals to set limits).

A change of scenery and some fresh air can do wonders, not only for students who have a lot of physical energy, but also for all of your students whose physical self can be suppressed in poorly ventilated, low lit rooms. Every once in a while, check to make sure the following elements are supporting the physical selves in your classroom:

Elements to Support the Physical Self in the Classroom

- Is the lighting sufficient? Rooms that are too dimly lit can cause drowsiness. Rooms that are too bright can cause difficulty in focusing and/or headaches.
- Is the temperature well suited for learning? Too hot and your students are falling asleep; too cold and they will be expending energy just trying to stay warm. On hot summer days, consider being outside in the shade. If your room is too cold, allow scarves, gloves, coats, and . . . blankets! Keep some old ones stashed in the corner.
- Is the room ventilated well? If it's too stuffy, open the windows to revive your students.
- Can your lectures be heard? Have a fellow teacher stand in the back of your classroom to see how well he can hear you. You may need to increase your volume or employ a microphone. Likewise, environmental noises may need to be managed (i.e., request that the lawn be cut after classroom hours).

CHAPTER SUMMARY

Check In With Your Self

When schools incorporate more physical education, mind/body awareness, sleep, and nutrition education, students will find more academic and life success.

____I totally disagree   _____Maybe agree a little   _____Yes, I agree
____I completely agree   _____Not only do I agree, but I'm going to do something about it!

Becoming aware of how all of these physical elements contribute to optimal functioning supports a shift in consciousness toward a healthier lifestyle and a stronger sense of self. Yes, simply knowing that

- sugar depletes brain power,
- physical activity increases cognitive performance,
- a poor night's sleep is crippling to test or athletic performance,
- visualizing the end goal helps achieve it, and
- restlessness can be a sign of a life's passion

empowers your students to take responsibility and set higher standards of personal achievement.

Interventions

Community resources: Variety at a limited cost

School teams

Activity breaks

Nutrition assignment

Time management

Create healthful habits

Visualization

Mindfulness

Meditation

Yoga

Activity: Incorporate the Physical Self When Possible

Situation	Goal	Intervention
Describe a situation you hope to improve.	What do you hope to achieve with the student?	Which intervention in the chapter will you use?
Mike has so much nervous energy he makes me nervous!	*I hope to be able to handle it better myself but also find ways for him to express his energy.*	*Allow Mike more opportunity to move during lessons. Discuss a plan to take "water breaks." Help him to feel accepted, nervous energy and all! Also, ask my team and principal about using some relaxation methods—mindfulness and meditation.*

Outcome
List the time frame and overall impressions.
He stood in the back of the class behind his desk and rocked back and forth while learning. He never interrupted. It only took me a couple days to adjust. He is definitely more focused, as am I! My team is on board with the mindfulness idea, but waiting to hear from the principal.

Now construct a chart from your experience.

The Self in the School Climate: Create an Environment That Works for You

Nobody cares how much you know, until they know how much you care.

—Theodore Roosevelt

WHAT YOU WILL LEARN IN THIS CHAPTER

This chapter covers Step 7: Create an environment that works for you and your students. In this chapter, you will learn

- What school climate is
- Personal principles of behavior
- Schoolwide policies
- Parents and the off-campus community

WHAT IS SCHOOL CLIMATE?

The way students feel and live in the classroom will affect how they retrieve information later (Brackett,

Check In With Your Self

Have you ever worked in a place where you didn't feel supported? Have you ever walked into a meeting where you felt the hostility of others? Have you ever experienced a group setting that was fraught with negativity? How did this affect your desire to participate?

Reyes, Rivers, Elbertson, & Salovey, 2011; Combs, 1997, 2010). Therefore, creating a safe atmosphere conducive to learning, behaving, connecting, and becoming a fully functioning member of society is a critical component of teaching to the self. School climate embodies the intended school ethos that resonates throughout the hallways and seeps into the very fiber of your student body consciousness, indeed your faculty consciousness.

School climate is the environment that *each school creates* to support student learning. It is equivalent to the atmosphere found in homes, businesses, and organizations across the globe. Every environment has subtle but authentic physical, emotional, and psychological elements. The spirit of that environment, the feeling that each person has about committing his or her time and effort within that setting, is a very palpable and real entity and sets the stage for the quality of work possible within it.

In fact, studies show (Brackett et al., 2011; Durlak, Weissberg, Dymnicki, Taylor, & Schellinger, 2011; Willis, 2011b) that when students are taught in an atmosphere conducive to sharing, acceptance, and self-exploration, information is more apt to resonate with the self, providing relevance and meaning. This connection with the material results in higher retention and less anxiety. Students also engage more with the material, feel more confident, and display more prosocial behavior. Hence, failure to address school climate will diminish your well-intended and hard-fought efforts at connection and growth.

School climate is like an eggshell: protective and delicate all at once. The interventions suggested here provide an extra layer of protection. Indeed, when a school climate is strong and built on years of hard work and consistent behavior, little will be able to crack its firm barrier, and your students will feel safe and protected. Incorporating the policies and principles herein enables the delicate nature of your students' "contents" to feel protected and limitless. An overall sense of community, and feelings of safety and connection, are necessary for your students to flourish.

We covered teamwork in Chapter 6, and indeed, a school could be considered one giant team working toward the growth of all students. But just how does one create a productive team when so many members are involved? It necessitates two elements: what the school expects and supports on a personal level *within its students* (and faculty) to promote that atmosphere and what *the school will provide* to achieve its intended climate. Let us begin with the personal principles of behavior that support a flourishing school climate.

PERSONAL PRINCIPLES OF BEHAVIOR

Four principles of behavior are discussed below. As you weave these elements into the ethos of your school via the interventions suggested, these principles of behavior, which strengthen a collaborative and community-minded atmosphere, will resonate within each and every student. The four that are essential to reaching the self are empathy, morality, self-control, and resilience.

Personal Principle of Behavior 1: Empathy

We touched on the importance of empathy in Chapter 4 in the discussion on bullying, but it warrants repeating as empathy is not only an antidote for bullying but also a key contributing personal principal to positive behavior within the classroom and throughout school. Empathy is what allows us to feel another person's pain, frustration, excitement, joy, or anxiety. When we understand how another person is feeling, we are better apt to adjust our responses accordingly. Imagine if you said to someone, "My dog just died," and she responded with, "One less mouth to feed!" You would likely feel a sense of disconnect. Empathy is what allows us to make appropriate assumptions about others' experiences. We know that losing a pet would make us sad (rather than elated at the decreased expenditure), and so, we offer words of condolences that help us to connect with the other person.

Our ability to tune into the state of mind of another person (empathy) depends in part on how well we are able to tune into our own. This resonance requires knowledge of who we are. We feel other people's feelings by actually feeling our own and then experiencing, at times, a sense of resonance with others. Connections with others are facilitated by the resonance found within ourselves. This is why a climate that supports the self is so important—when we are in touch with our selves, we are more likely to experience empathy and, thus, to forge connections, both of which improve school climate.

> Empathy is a main avenue to connection. When your students are connected to each other, they are more likely to help each other learn rather than withdraw or disconnect from the process.

Intervention 8.1: Model Empathy

Though some people seem to lack empathy, it can be built through practice. Continually ask students who are disruptive, aggressive, or hurtful to others how they would have felt had they been the recipient of their own actions. (Listen for a feeling in the response, not a thought. Help students connect to the feelings.) However, when you do this, model empathy for them: "Now that you are sitting in the hallway waiting for detention because you hit Jesse for the third time this week, I guess you might be feeling that life is a bit unfair and that you seem to get all the punishment and not Jesse. Is that right?" Seek to connect with their feelings. Once they feel heard—a deep need for all humans—they are more likely to "hear" others. The experience of empathy from another can help foster one's own empathy.

Another way to connect via empathy is to remember the axiom: Seek first! When handling a situation where a child has been disruptive or has bullied someone, find reasons why, in his eyes, he did what he did. Come alongside him and seek his perspective. Listen first.

We are all born with the capacity for empathy, but it needs continual support and encouragement to grow and become solidified as part of the self. The more we empathize with others, the more we take their needs and desires into consideration. This is why cultivating empathy in your school climate is so vital. Students with empathy begin to see the repercussions their actions have not just on themselves but also on their fellow students and on you. Empathy can only grow, however, when it is nurtured in an environment that is rich with empathy itself.

Personal Principle of Behavior 2: Morality

Moral reasoning is the ability to distinguish right from wrong. Moral behavior stems from being aware of the principles you value and in which order you place them. Having a strong sense of self enables us to live up to those convictions.

> The philosopher Descartes has been quoted as saying, "Although each of us is a person distinct from all others . . . we must always remember that none of us could exist alone. . . . The interests of the whole, of which each of us is part, must always be preferred to those of our individual personality" (Kagan, 1984, p. 116).

Young children focus on consequences related to morality: *I did something wrong, so now I will be in trouble.* The young teen, however, has a budding level of insight, so the moral focus shifts to intentions. *Who am I in this situation? What impression do I want to leave? How will that impact my reputation? What is the "right" thing to do?* On top of this, teens are often sent multiple messages from multiple sources. *My friends think I should do this, my parents think I should do that, my boyfriend wants one thing, and my religious convictions say another.* This is why discussing and exploring morality on a personal level cultivates a strong school environment where intentions are discussed, consequences understood, and purposes aligned. Nurturing the innate moral sense of each student solidifies the self and increases prosocial behavior. This is turn elevates the entire school climate.

School is ripe with opportunities to weave moral lessons into the day. What school hasn't discussed the ethics of bullying? Cheating? Skipping class? Disruptive behavior? Every day, schools face challenges that provide a fertile ground for developing the moral code of each student. How readily we recognize and grasp those opportunities depends on the commitment we have to developing respect, concern, accountability, kindness, honesty—all the elements we identify with "character." Each of those elements contribute to your school atmosphere—when they are celebrated and shared by all, the climate of the school becomes ripe for learning.

Consider a Code of Conduct

Does your school have a code of conduct? How is it discussed? Agreed upon? Followed? Is it punitive or supportive? Were students part of its development? Does every student *and faculty member* read it and abide by it (by signing it)? If not, consider implementing a schoolwide code of conduct policy. Meet with students and discuss what principles they believe should guide the students *and faculty* at the school.

Intervention 8.2: Debate Moral Dilemmas

Perhaps a recent event in the news or at school is the perfect subject for your students. Common moral discussions include the ethical considerations as to why a straight *A* student might cheat or why a star baseball player might experiment with steroid use. If you are at a loss, you can find a host of moral dilemmas to discuss here: www.goodcharacter.com/dilemma/dilemma.html.

My Favorite Moral Dilemmas by Charis Denison, founder of Prajna Consulting and an expert in Community Involvement, Human Development and Ethics.

Charis provides a list of moral dilemmas—31 as of this printing. Below are introductions to her top three. On the site, you will click on the introduction to read the whole story. Notes for the facilitator (you) and discussion questions are also provided.

1. The star student makes a bad choice involving alcohol. Now she has to decide what to do about it without ruining her reputation or compromising her ethical principles.

2. What do you do when your friend's dad comes to drive you home from a party, and you can tell that he's drunk?

3. Katy cringes every time she hears her friends use words like "retarded" or "gay" in a derogatory manner. Should she object when it happens, or should she let it pass so people won't think she's weird?

Personal Principle of Behavior 3: Self-Control

Policies, interventions, and cultural practices aimed at bolstering self-control may improve the welfare of the general population rather than just a subset of severely impaired individuals.

—Duckworth (2011, p. 2639)

Self-control is discussed in Chapter 5 as a cognitive ability that helps alleviate stress. Here we discuss self-control as it relates specifically to refraining from acting out or becoming distracted in the classroom and beyond. Learning is thwarted when teens act out or even just call out of turn. Imagine if even 10% of your population began to control impulsive behavior; how might school climate shift?

Indeed, lack of self-control is a contributing factor to many of the problems that plague not just your classroom, but modern society as a whole—addiction, overeating, overspending, domestic abuse, violent crime, unsafe sex, failure to exercise, falling off a task (homework or work). Self-control has been cited as producing a broad range of benefits. Research done on self-control (Moffit et al., 2010) has found that when one is able to control temptation, profound benefits include financial security, physical and mental health, a reduction in substance abuse and criminality, and improved income. The good news is that self-control can be strengthened in everyone.

Self-control is like a muscle: It grows stronger with repeated use (and can fatigue if tested too long; think of will power fading after a long time on a diet). To increase it, Baumeister recommends overriding habitual ways of doing things and exerting deliberate control over your actions such as brushing your teeth or opening doors with your nondominant hand (Weir, 2012).

Tasks can be more goal directed as well. In your classroom, this might translate to sitting still for increasing lengths of time, getting up slowly when the bell rings, or pausing 3 seconds before speaking.

> Self-control requires glucose. To help boost your students' performance on self-control tasks, offer them a glass of lemonade beforehand, suggests Baumeister (same article as above).

Moreover, Baumeister, during his studies in the 1990s, concluded that mental challenges sap self-control energy. For instance, if students are stressed over an exam, Baumeister found that they would be more likely to give in to impulses than students who did not have an exam. These findings correlate with the theme of this book: When students are taxed emotionally and/or mentally, impulses and poor decisions dominate. By helping them manage their demanding environments and internal worlds, we help them become more productive, increase impulse control, and support good decisions. Of note, one of the main strategies that Baumeister found to bolster impulse control was self-awareness. Tips for increasing self-control include the following:

- Increase awareness of the risks association with the impulse.
- Talk about your goals, both to affirm intention and seek support.
- Create if-then steps (see Intervention 8.3: Chunk and Reward).
- Be nice to your self along the way.
- Change your thinking about the impulse (for example, a cookie may become a gateway to diabetes or cancer rather than a reward for achieving a task).
- Avoid situations that bring out the worst in you.
- Destress so impulse control is fortified.

(Some of the tips in the list above were adapted from the article "Control Yourself" in *Scientific American Mind*, May/June 2011, by Hofmann, W. and Friese, M., p. 45.)

The Drawback of Affluence

In Paul Tough's (2012) book *How Children Succeed,* he compared the character development of affluent students with those from low socio-economic backgrounds. Those from affluent communities are often parent protected and rarely experience failure. This results in lower levels of grit and self-control. Children from less affluent homes, on the other hand, who have struggled and often faced repeated obstacles, develop the passion and perseverance (self-control) to succeed in the face of tremendous strife. In essence, he says, kids need to learn how to fail if they are to succeed.

Intervention 8.3: Chunk and Reward

Since self-control is like a muscle, breaking things down into smaller tasks helps to combat fatigue. For instance, instead of having to run 5 miles, an individual can run a mile five times—an easier task to accomplish. To capitalize on this aspect in developing self-control, have students define their goals for the day, week, month, or year (your choice). Let's say a student's goals for the week include studying for a math final on Friday and completing half the team project assignment. After making the list, ask him to plan *how* he will reach these goals. What are his strategies as far as scheduling and time management? Have the students break down their goals into small achievable steps. Then have them actually check off their lists as they complete each step. The physical act of checking off completed tasks is a highly persuasive psychological method for feeling a sense of reward and accomplishment. Next, have students weave reward systems into their plans. When they have been diligent as far as tasks (*If I complete my math packet by 7 . . .*), they can reward themselves with something fun (*. . . then I will take an iChat break for 15 minutes*). This routine sets up positive self-control habits for life (particularly because the brain is wiring for habits during this time and "if/then" thinking flexes prefrontal cortex [PFC] functions).

Check In With Your Self

How does your classroom climate promote learning from mistakes, rather than feeling shamed by them?

Personal Principle of Behavior 4: Resilience

A close cousin to self-control is resilience: the ability to handle setbacks, to not just weather them but to learn and grow from them.

Determination and will power sustain us when the going gets tough. Resilience is often cited as the key component in success, surpassing other variables such as IQ or education level (Tough, 2012). But just how do you build it? Some children naturally have more resilience than others: *Johnny always cried when he didn't get his way; Lorenzo always figured out how to make his way happen even when told no.* Is it innate? To some extent yes. Some flowers are certainly hardier by nature. But can it be built? Without question. Resilience is a skill that can be developed, blossoming fully, just like the delicate rose that survives the storm.

One way to nurture this ability in your students is to focus on the effort of your students rather than the outcome. In Carol Dweck's influential work *Mindset* (2006), she describes several experiments in which groups of children were either praised for their effort on a task—*Hey! That was a tough problem. You did great! You must have worked very hard*—or praised for their "smarts"—*Hey! You must be very smart.* Consistently, children who were praised for being smart became reluctant to take greater risks. If getting the problem right meant they were smart, then conversely, getting a problem wrong might threaten that label: wrong became "not smart." However, the students who were praised for their effort were not only willing to take greater risks, but they also enjoyed doing so. They found challenging problems fun. Getting something wrong did not threaten the state of the self. Getting something wrong meant more effort needed to be applied—something every child praised for his or her effort believed he or she could do.

A school climate that values effort over outcome is one that supports limitless potential and builds resilience. When the focus is on grades and how "smart" they are, students freeze in the uncertainty of not having what it takes to succeed. Yet, the ability to apply effort is unfettered—everyone, no matter how gifted or "smart," can always apply effort. When the focus is on effort, students feel empowered; they become resilient to setbacks.

The overriding message from teachers, principals, and coaches alike that supports resilience is one that focuses on effort—*How hard did you try? Did you put your best effort forward? When you encountered difficulty, did you stay the course?* Report cards that remark on effort may help to shift the ethos of the school. Effort reports send the message—*We care about how hard you work. We want you to fulfill your potential.* Students who possess more resilience see mistakes as opportunities for growth rather than a fault in themselves (i.e., *I am not smart*).

Teacher Illustration 8.1: Building Resilience

Donna Volpitta, EdD, is a resilience educator and author of The Resilience Formula: A Guide to Proactive, Not Reactive, Parenting. *Below she provides an overview of her approach.*

"I can't do it! It's too hard!"

"He cut in front of me in line!"

"She said he wasn't going to be my friend."

"They wouldn't let me play."

Everyone faces challenges.

Our resilience is how we respond to those challenges, big or small, and those responses are based on our understanding of four *S*s:

Self: Our knowledge about our self and our reactions

Situation: Our judgments about the given challenging situations

Support: Our ability to access support systems if we need help

Strategies: The specific strategies that we are able to use to handle the challenge

Kids need resilience. They need to learn how to handle challenge themselves because it is through learning how to handle those small challenges that they begin to develop an understanding of those four *S*s that will help them to handle the larger challenges that will present themselves. Because our resilience for any challenge is based on those four *S*s, teachers can use small challenges to teach resilience skills, enabling their students to be better prepared to handle the bigger challenges.

Metacognitive skills—the ability to think about their own thinking—are critical for students to develop the first two *S*s: self and situation. Teachers can actively incorporate lessons that guide students to think about themselves: who they are, what they stand for, and what their strengths and weaknesses are. Similarly, teachers can guide their students in the ability to judge a situation, scaffolding their ability to gain perspective.

Through everyday challenges, teachers can teach the second two *S*s: supports and strategies. As teachers, our initial reaction is to solve problems. Instead, we need to teach how to solve problems, giving our students the tools that they need to solve those problems on their own.

Intervention 8.4: Pretests and Rewrites

Test taking is a necessary and realistic life skill, but it is not the journey if the destination is true learning, mastering, and applying. So take the time to teach in a way that supports a resilient-blossoming self. Provide pretests to allow your students to see where their shortcomings lie. Allow them to rewrite papers to increase their grades. Return to theories and ideas until they become old hat. Ask the same questions in different ways until the answers become second nature. Research consistently tells us that when students fail at *small* tasks, they develop resilience and the conviction to get back into the saddle (Brooks & Goldstein, 2003). Students who never face failure are less likely to be able to cope with it when it does happen.

Attempting something that is risky and that may lead to failure breeds character, creativity, resilience, and perseverance. But a belief in the self and a growth mindset are prerequisites for those attempts not to backfire (Dweck, 2006; Tough, 2012). In fact, the more risk you take, the more the feeling of success, even when you need to "chunk" your achievements to attain success. Remember, those synapses and tracks of the self are being formed—as well as being aggressively pruned—during the teen years. Thus, this is the time for teens to learn that making mistakes is okay. What matters is managing the event (as well as the accompanying feelings), getting back on task, trying again, and thinking of new and creative solutions. When you help students realize that they can rebound after mistakes or a perceived failure, you build their self-concepts and you teach important life skills such as commitment, patience, determination, decision making, and problem solving. You demonstrate to them that failure is a part of life and can help them to make progress. Build into your atmosphere the idea that *mistakes will be made. What will you make of them?*

Teacher Illustration 8.2: Allowing Failure

Amy Smith, English Teacher, Ramapo High School, Franklin Lakes, NJ

I have always thought that there was something very wrong about giving a writing assignment to students with the expectation that the students would fulfill the requirements of that assignment and turn in finely tuned papers. In any other subject, the students learn a concept, practice it to become proficient, and are finally tested. Writing assignments, for the most part, don't allow for practice. The students usually have to submit their assignments on the "due date" and wait for their teachers to return them with their grades. They rarely, if ever, have the chance to practice the skill of writing. The strong students almost always receive high grades, while those who struggle with their writing almost always fail. Most important, they usually don't know why. They just know they "can't write."

With that in mind, I decided to establish the portfolio system of writing in my classroom. I would give the students a writing assignment and, at the same time, give them a "final due date." Between the date I gave the assignment and the final due date, the students could submit their papers as often as they wanted, many times conferencing with me about their work. I would highlight areas that needed work or correction, and they would rewrite and submit again. By the time the due date arrived, some students had submitted their papers four or five times. I met with them as many times as possible, but I encouraged peer reviewing, which many times took the onus off me. What I found was the students who usually failed had the incentive to try again and again and again if necessary. By allowing them to correct their poor writing, and affording them the possibility of ultimately receiving a high grade, they not only kept trying, they also improved their writing each time. When some of those students received their *A+*, the pride on their faces was palpable. This was a true win-win situation.

The above example shows how enriching learning from and handling errors can be. Rather than have students receive a final paper riddled with red marks, Smith (teacher) used scaffolding to help build their writing techniques. As such, the neuronal tracks of *I can't do anything right* were avoided and new tracks of *I can do this* were supported and resilience built. Students also developed skills for time management and planning ahead—important executive functions. Schools that present mistakes as learning opportunities create an environment where students can take risks, stumble, and still succeed. A climate that fosters resilience empowers students to persevere in school and in life.

SCHOOLWIDE POLICIES

Schoolwide policies create a common vision and purpose across your entire student body. When schools have faculty that model the code of conduct, an atmosphere that is bursting with pride, a sense of community that is strong and safe, and a sense of gratitude that is felt by all, those schools are primed to reach, nurture, and protect every student's sense of self.

The atmosphere we allow says a lot about who we are as educators and what we expect from our students. Take for example this scenario: Imagine being in a meeting with your principal. You arrive a few minutes late because a student had an emergency and needed 5 minutes of your time. Your principal admonishes you (without seeking an explanation first), scowls at you (nonverbal communication), and points to a chair implying you take a seat (disrespect). With negativity looming, you sense your principal about to unleash a wrath of concerns (freezing occurs—you are anxious and stressed). She asks you a series of questions that you fluster through because you can't seem to focus (PFC has shut down). When asked whether or not you had done a particular deed, you can't recall (hippocampus shut down—memory flustered). You leave the meeting unsure of your job security (feelings unworthy, self-doubt) and begin to tremble (cortisol unleashed in your system, wreaking havoc). You go home and pour a drink (bad habit?).

Can you relate to this story?

How might your students be able to relate?

When emotions are not valued, the atmosphere is oppressive.

Schoolwide Policy 1: Faculty Conduct

Today my math teacher told us that if we couldn't solve the problem on the board, we should all hang our heads in shame.

—Student, age 14

A code of conduct can never reach its potential if those in leadership positions do not abide by those principles themselves. Unfortunately, in some schools, one set of rules exists for the teachers and one set of rules for the students. Faculty ask that students treat each other respectfully, and yet, as the quote above illustrates, they often publicly shame students. Some teachers expect that students listen to them and then they ignore the students' requests for one-on-one time. Some ask students to complete assignments on time and then fail to return graded papers in the same timely fashion. We ask that students show empathy for each other, and yet we often fail to empathize with what it means to be a teen struggling with identity formation, peer pressure, and a digital world that has no predecessor or filter.

Practicing what the school code preaches is not just a matter of fairness; it is a way for educators to model what emotional management looks like. In order to promote a code of conduct in your students, teachers and staff must live it moment to moment in the classroom, hallways, and sports fields even when times are tough. Who are you when the storm hits? Of course, being the calm in the middle of the storm will greatly benefit you and your students. They need a model to see in action what is expected of them: That it can be done. The behavior you exhibit and ask of your class says, *This is how I expect you to be—fair and considerate of all.* It is a powerful tool in creating a positive schoolwide climate.

Schoolwide Policy 2: Morale

Check In With Your Self

What is it like to walk down your hallways, attend a sporting event, enter the cafeteria, or sit in the common areas? What energy is present? How do you and other faculty members contribute to that energy?

Building school morale builds students' connections with the school and with others. What does your school do to encourage morale? Creating social activities that boost school spirit and encourage participation elevates the possibility of social connection for, and increases motivation among, your students. When possible:

- Have special events, such as dances and carnivals, at the school grounds.
- Enlist students in fundraisers to improve parts of the school they enjoy the most, such as the sports fields or art room.
- Have fun "competitions" between homerooms.
- Put up large posters depicting student life.
- Create "interesting" school days such as pajama day, tied-to-a-buddy day, crazy hat day, etc.
- Check in with students on their sense of school pride: What do they cherish? What do they not like?
- Surround students with their artwork, inspirational quotes, thought-provoking questions, so hallways and cafeterias are not bare and boring.
- Tell students you are proud of the school: Let them hear it, let them see it with your words and actions.

Common sense and our intuition reveal that the more positive students feel *toward* their school, the more productive and happy they will be *in* their school. School morale increases the sense of connection, and the greater the sense of connection and emotional attachment to school, the lower the dropout rate (Sroufe, Egeland, Carlson, & Collins, 2005). Do you know how your students feel about their school? What does the morale feel like to them? If you don't know, ask. Just polling your students about their school morale can help to bring it into focus and begin the process of strengthening it.

> Lest we forget, most students face a daily reality something like this (or worse): get up at 6 a.m., make the bus by 7, work all day, avoid social stressors constantly, return home for dinner, cram all night, get little sleep, and wake up and do it again. Does your school climate honor that effort?

Intervention 8.5: Project-Based Learning to Enhance School Morale

Project-based learning can be applied to nearly any lesson. In this case, create teams of students to evaluate and think critically about school morale. Is it a problem in the school? How do students perceive their school? Has this changed over time? How do they wish the morale to be in their school? Have students work together to track and evaluate the information. Once information is gathered, have students meet in focus groups to analyze the meanings and discover possible solutions. You may choose to have them represent the findings visually in graphs, diagrams, or charts. They are then responsible for implementing those solutions and tracking the results—again using a visual aid. What helped? What didn't? Simply by working together to find a solution, morale may be improved.

Schoolwide Policy 3: Develop a Sense of Community

Developing morale will go a long way toward creating a sense of community; indeed, they almost go hand in hand. However, a sense of community goes beyond school pride. Community building helps students realize the impact their actions have on a greater whole. It teaches them that they are connected to many people and that their actions have far-reaching effects. Moreover, when a sense of community exists, students are more apt to help each other and show compassion during tough times—social skills that will serve them well both outside school and throughout their lives.

Here are a few examples of how to foster a sense of community with your students:

Schedule Weekly Meetings

Schedule weekly meetings to discuss topics relevant to your particular class (fundraising efforts, a trip, group work that isn't working, etc.). These may not be part of *your* agenda but may be part of *theirs*. By opening up the dialogue, you develop a sense that everyone in the community matters and everyone has a chance to be heard. This can also be done online.

Seek Whole-School Feedback

Seek feedback on issues before making changes that will affect the student body. For example, to foster a sense of community if funds are only available for either a new sports field or instruments for band, ask the students how they feel about the two choices. Given the opportunity to be heard and involved, they may even come up with fundraising strategies to accomplish both. Bringing these topics to their attention promotes a 21st century skills mindset because it encourages a group mentality, a sense of community, creative thinking, innovation, and collaboration.

Ask Students for Input and Create Traditions

Are students part of decisions on how to improve school morale and climate? Is there a social issue prevalent in your school? How is the school managing it? Might you need help from the student body? Furthermore, what traditions have your students started? What traditions make your classroom special? Traditions bring a group together while promoting community spirit. Traditions are emotional and resonate with those involved. How can you begin a tradition today? Why not ask students for input?

Morning Announcements

Nearly all schools have an intercom system whereby morning announcements are delivered, the Pledge of Allegiance is honored, and sometimes music is played. With the same routine each morning (except perhaps for the occasional tantalizing bake sale announcement), how can students transform from robotic passive listeners to superheroes of community engagement? Try mixing in a little scavenger hunt or a password for the day, which, when all the passwords for the week are remembered, wins those students a visit to the principal (Imagine that? Without a punishment!) to retrieve their prize. Better yet, increase learning skills using the same technique: Have the word of the day mixed in with your subject content and see if hands go up when you mention the word—who's paying attention now? The prize need not be huge, but the interaction and positive praise for finding the clue or hearing the password amid a teacher lecture on pathogens of the 17th century is rewarding in and of itself.

Gratitude Themes

Develop academic and community service-minded gratitude themes. Each month, students collectively vote on what they choose to honor and how they will honor it. This could coincide with national themes: November is a time to appreciate veterans or to give thanks; January we appreciate a chance to start fresh; April is an appreciation for life. Students will work collaboratively and feel a sense of community during the voting process itself. As they work together to find ways to honor the theme of the month, they will likely benefit from an "other" minded focus. Indeed, doing a kindness for another person produces the single most reliable increase in happiness of anything studied thus far (Seligman, 2011). That is, when we help another, we feel happier than when we receive a gift, buy something, or play our favorite sport. Gratitude and caring for others increases our sense of self, brings purpose to our lives and community to our schools.

Schoolwide Policy 4: School Safety

Absenteeism strongly contributes to poor academic performance, dropout rates, and a lack of connection with staff (Balfanz & Byrnes, 2012; Brown, 2012). This is why schools work hard to get students to school, as well as keep them safe in school. Many children fear merely traveling to and from school safely. Simply walking or taking transportation to and from school can be a deterrent to many students, as many of them face issues such as drugs, crime, or peer pressure. As you consider your school safety policies, please consider school routes, arrival and dismissal times, and the intricacies of simply going from one place to another. Working with local officials, improving road conditions, lighting pathways, and increasing police patrols at the right times can all aid a student's sense of safety before she even arrives.

Concern about safety at school can distract the cognitive flow and send reflexes to the reactive areas of the brain, jettisoning learning potential faster than your students change fashions. All the interventions in this book have the ultimate aim of allowing each self to feel safe—socially, cognitively, emotionally, and physically—in your school.

Students are aware of the tragedy that occurred at the Sandy Hook Elementary School. What are the steps your school has taken to instill a feeling of safety? Were children involved in, or informed of, the subsequent decisions/actions taken? Of course with a consideration to age-appropriate content, letting students know that you have taken every precaution possible, and allowing them to voice their fears, ideas, and emotions will help alleviate their anxiety levels. Whenever a tragedy occurs that speaks directly to their sense of safety (whether it is local, national, or international), ignoring their input and concerns compromises that sense of safety. School-to-parent communication is paramount during these times.

School Bomb Threats

Some teens find making threats to the school a means of entertainment and a potential way to delay upcoming tests. When a bomb threat succeeds in distracting the school schedule, everyone loses—police, ambulance, fire fighters, community members, parents, teachers, and students. Of course you must follow procedure, but when students do return, try a project-based learning activity that promotes empathy and considers consequences. What is the cost/benefit to society, parents, and municipal workers when a bomb threat occurs? What might a person who calls in a bomb threat be going through? How can the school and the student body proactively and collaboratively work toward eliminating threats altogether? A punitive reaction may only fuel the fire for more threats, whereas working together creatively to make sure every student feels safe may reduce threats going forward.

In Summary

Implementing schoolwide policies that engage students and make learning as well as school participation enjoyable and personally meaningful inspires creativity, connection, and collaboration. These elements of your school environment can often be more difficult to implement, as they require a common vision among all of your faculty members and personnel. However, the effort in building school morale and a strong sense of community will reap its rewards tenfold. When students feel pride, community, and a sense of safety in their school, school becomes an extended family: a place where they can grow and reach their potentials.

PARENTS AND THE OFF-CAMPUS COMMUNITY

Navigating parental desires can be as tricky as navigating some of your teens. Some parents seem to believe they could run your classroom much better than you (despite their lack of experience), and other parents don't seem to care what you do—or their children do—in your classroom. However, active parental involvement in monitoring schoolwork and the parents' clear expectations have been shown to positively impact students' desire for higher education (Simon, 2001). Thus, parents can very much be your allies in the classroom (without them actually being there, of course!).

Working with families has been considered difficult because it is fraught with emotions: *How dare you tell me how to raise my child!* Or even denial (a defense): *My son would never do anything like that!* But much like we've taught you about defenses with students, interventions work well with parents, too. Remember to come alongside: "I see Franco has missed school a lot this semester." (Object oriented—the discussion is about missing school, not parenting.) "Getting to school is challenging sometimes when so much else is happening." (This is validating, not accusing.) "How can the school work more efficiently to meet Franco's needs and help him get to school on time?" (This takes responsibility away from the parent and releases defenses so communication can take place.) Then gently remind parents (affirming what may or may not be happening) that their involvement is very much appreciated and indeed helpful toward shaping their child's outcome: A subliminal suggestion indeed, but one with powerful repercussions when delivered delicately.

In addition, reach out to parents about the positive things their child has done. For many parents, especially those raising more challenging children, a phone call home means something has gone wrong (yet again). Imagine the possibilities when you call to admire something about their child? "Hello Mrs. Warner, I just want to let you know that Aldo did something very kind in class today. He shared his reading book with Guam without having to be asked. I wanted you to know that I really appreciated Aldo's kind spirit today." The next time you do have to make a more "negative" phone call to Aldo's parents, they will be more likely to see you as someone who appreciates their child and therefore may be more willing to hear what you have to say.

Teacher Illustration 8.3: Building Positive Connections With Parents

Lorraine Skeen, Retired Principal of Patrick Henry School, P.S. 171, New York, NY

During the years I served as a principal, I observed that certain teachers contacted parents about good news and were lavish in their praise when students persevered. The parents in turn were extremely cooperative when these teachers said there was a problem and they needed the parents' help.

Moreover, systematic outreach to parents by teachers supports academic success and psychological well-being. Not to use this tool is to deny students a support that is essential, one that allows them to function on their highest level.

CHAPTER SUMMARY

> **Check In With Your Self**
>
> When was the last time you made a call home to tell a parent something positive about his or her child? How often do you call home to discuss "problematic" behaviors?

Interventions

Model empathy

Debate moral dilemmas

Chunk and reward

Pretests and rewrites

Project-based learning to enhance school morale

Other than the interventions above, schoolwide policy ideas include: consider faculty conduct, improve morale, poll your students, develop a sense of community (seek whole-school feedback, ask students for input and create traditions, morning assignments, gratitude themes), use project-based learning, and consider school safety.

Activity: Improve School Climate

(Note: This chart has been altered to accommodate chapter content.)

Situation	Goal	Intervention
Describe a situation you hope to improve.	What do you hope to achieve?	Which intervention in the chapter will you use?
The morale in our school has hit a real low.	*More involvement on the part of the faculty and students to improve morale and general atmosphere in the school.*	*Index cards, project-based learning, poll students, morning announcement ideas, and gratitude themes. I also have some other ideas relevant to my community.*

Outcome
List the time frame and overall impressions.
I plan to bring other faculty on board—this will take a few weeks. Then I want to hear from students and assess the situation—gain some insight. That will take another few weeks. I would like to include a project-based learning around this idea and hope other teachers will support it.
It's only been a month, but already the school has new energy—just the idea of evaluating and fixing the morale has boosted spirits.

Now construct a chart from your experience.

9

The Self: Decision Making, Motivation, and Giving Back

Educating the mind without educating the heart is no education at all.

—Aristotle

WHAT YOU WILL LEARN IN THIS CHAPTER

This chapter covers

- Where are we? (Fear, job preparedness, personal connections, financial impact)
- Where can we go from here? (Decision making, motivation, giving back)
- Final interventions (Self Folder, celebrate the self, incorporate social emotional learning [SEL])

WHERE ARE WE?

Entire books have been written on the "current" state of education. Research studies come out weekly on children's mental health issues. Here we outline only a few relevant considerations (fear, job preparedness, personal connections, and financial impact) as we peek at where we are before we look at where we can go.

Where We Are: Fear

Learning is an emotional event, impacted by how you're feeling. . . . You can't grasp new information in a state of fear. Punishment and threats actually inhibit the learning process

(Pert, 2006, p. 49).

Fear is an impediment to motivation and ultimate success. Where does it creep into your students' lives, and how does it affect their academic and life performance? We create a fear-based childhood when we compete for better grades and test scores, when we focus on results rather than the effort and the process, or when we punish children too severely. The fear becomes stress and anxiety, which depresses learning potential, leads to varied physical and mental health issues, and yet, still we provide little to no coping strategies.

> **Check In With Your Self**
>
> What do you think your students' fear-o-meter would read?
>
> __Off the charts   __Slightly   __Cool as
>   afraid   fearful   cucumbers

Forty million Americans suffer from fear disorders (LeDoux, 2002). We mention this because it underscores the importance of managing emotions, regulating your self socially, and making decisions based from conscious awareness—not from fear. Why are we so fearful? Many people will say they feel that they are not worthy enough, good enough, pretty enough, smart enough, talented enough, and so forth. They fear admonishment, shame, bullying, heartache, loss, transition, and much more. They fear that their selves will be judged and found lacking with the ultimate result of rejection by others (disconnection).

Brene Brown gave a TED talk (Brown, 2011) in which she describes the harsh reality of people who do not feel worthy (and it plagues most of us!). She says that courage, connection, compassion, and the capacity for vulnerability lead us from this shame state (where we usually end up numbing ourselves: overeating, cutting, bullying, becoming indebted, and addicted more than ever). But she says that the children raised with a strong sense of self are most likely to feel worthy. Thank you, Brene. For those of you who haven't had the privilege of hearing her, the *intervention* here would be to watch her discussion. Please visit www.ted.com/talks/brene_brown_on_vulnerability.html. The defenses we presented to you in Chapter 3 are very much alive in your classroom today precisely because of the issue Brene addresses: We tend to hide our shame. Teaching to and supporting the self breaks the vicious cycle of shame (the fear that one is not worthy of connection) and defense (protection). As you nurture the self, the self feels safe enough so that real growth can take place.

Where We Are: Job Preparedness

> One of two students who starts college doesn't complete college. When asked why, they said they don't have study skills, know how to write, or know how to form a study group (Wagner, 2011).

Businesses need people who are creative, dependable, self-motivated, and innovative—all the things this book promotes, but not what all schools support. How are we preparing students to "innovate" when we are teaching them to solve standardized problems rather than asking them to think outside the box to solve real-time, community-based problems via, for example, project-based learning? Creativity and innovation are unleashed when students feel comfortable with themselves and not stuck solely in their left brains.

Moreover, rarely will you see an executive meeting in which everyone sits in rows as in a traditional classroom. People work *together.* Why aren't we learning *together?* To address this issue alone, we need to both rethink the competition ethos that is prevalent in most schools today as well as to actively seek the opportunities for students to work well together. Both of these changes, along with a focus on more innovative thinking, support the self for a future that places us back in the running as a globally competitive nation.

You may recall the eighth-grade physics teacher's e-mail to his class (Chapter 6) of "engineers." This is his comment to a parent about his overall philosophy:

> By the end of the year, most parents get it—this is not really about physics. It's about how we can work together to accomplish some monumentally challenging task—designing a nuclear powered research submarine. And on the way, could we be nice to each other? If they learn anything, I hope it's that. Once they have survived this grueling process, they seem to have the confidence that they can do anything. And they pretty much can. (Charles Duveen)

His approach is to be applauded—it isn't just about teaching physics (which he does quite well). It is about teamwork, social skills, and rising to a complex challenge, skills every child will need to compete in the labor world of tomorrow.

Check In With Your Self

What percentage of adults you know are not happy with their jobs or their relationships? (Before you continue to the next sentence, please answer this question for yourself.) This is a question we have asked hundreds of students. Every single time we ask it, *at least 75%* of students raise their hands.

Where We Are: Personal Connections

Our ability to effectively connect with each other is diminishing rapidly, and yet our current school protocol is not addressing the emotional impact of this reality. Because relationships fall outside the scope of traditional "education," we stand paralyzed as our youth struggle with the consequences.

Let's explore how the current state of connection and relationships contribute to our nation's overall health:

- 50% of marriages in this country end in divorce. America is among the top 10 countries with the highest divorce rate (www.divorcerate.org).
- 1 in 4 women have experienced domestic violence (Domestic Violence Statistics, 2013).
- 41% of marriages have a partner who reports infidelity, either emotional or physical ("Infidelity Statistics," 2006).
- Single parent families have become the norm for many within our country: 31% of children live in a single parent household (Kiefer, 2004).

Ignoring these problems, or saying that they shouldn't be our problem, won't fix the problem. The problem is real, and the fact remains that *schools are in the best position today to provide a solution:* to model solid, dependable, and caring relationships, and to provide teens with the self skills necessary to forge beautiful, respectful, and working relationships in the future. By reaching and teaching to the self and by polishing those containers, you empower kids to treat each other better and to feel more worthy. Indeed, a self skills approach has far-reaching implications for the successful personal lives of our students and the culture of our nation.

Where We Are: Financially

The costs when we lose students cannot be measured in financial terms alone. The emotional toil, the repercussions on family and community, and the loss of purpose and potential are all

---

Check In With Your Self

How much do you think we should spend on a curriculum to help students learn about themselves? What value would you place on a program that develops strong identities in students? Or that creates a proactive mindset? Or, one that has the potential to mitigate mental health concerns?

_____Zero. I haven't fallen for a word of this.

_____Less than major subjects like reading and mathematics

_____Equal amount of money that is spent on core curriculums

_____More than core curriculums—it's invaluable.

real and devastating losses. But often in today's world we are asked to put a price on matters before someone will take notice and deem something cost effective. The statistics of student drop out—most often caused by a lack of connection and poor decision making (a self skill)—are staggering:

- The combined income and tax losses from a *single year's dropouts* is about $192 *billion* (Milliken, 2007).
- Three-quarters of state prison inmates are dropouts, and 59% of federal prisoners are (Martin & Halperin, 2006).
- If 33% of dropouts would instead graduate from high school, the federal government would save $10.8 billion each year in food stamps, housing assistance, and temporary assistance for needy families (Martin & Halperin, 2006).

Furthermore, basic costs for troubled teens are sky-high:

- In the state of California, the Department of Juvenile Justice spent $119,880 in 2005 and then $216,081 in 2008 to incarcerate *one person per year* (Urban Strategies Council, 2007).

But how much do we allocate for mental health issues and violent crime?

- Antianxiety and antidepression medication use is at an all time high. Anxiety disorders alone cost the United States more than $42 billion a year (Anxiety and Depression Association of America, 2012). 50% of Americans will suffer from a mental health issue at some point in their lifetime ("A Neglect of Mental Illness," 2012).
- Left untreated, "Mental illnesses in the U.S. cost more than $100 billion a year in lost productivity, according to the National Alliance on Mental Illness." Teenagers are at risk, and more and more schools are increasing their special education classes ("A Neglect of Mental Illness," 2012).
- Forty-two billion dollars was also the price tag on violent crimes in America, crimes that result from anger, frustration, loss of hope, and the inability to control one's emotions (self factors) (Shapiro & Hassett, 2012).

And just how does one financially measure teen suicide? Homelessness? Lost dreams? Wasted potential? We don't believe one can. Or that one should.

In Summary

Our nation has a mental health crisis resulting, at times, in unfathomable atrocities. The costs when we fail to connect with our students and reach their selves cannot really be measured. Yet, the numbers make one thing abundantly clear: We need to reallocate our resources and our focus from a reactive system to a proactive one. When we make connections and nurture the self, then we can shift from fear to hope, prepare our students for careers of the future, promote positive fulfilling relationships, and stop spending an exorbitant amount of money on reactive measures.

WHERE CAN WE GO FROM HERE?

Education has the capacity to help students shift from a fear-based mentality to one that makes clear decisions and is motivated, repositioning us toward a helpful, community-minded, self-honoring system. Indeed, your reading this book is the first step in moving our education system in that direction. The ideas presented here provide a foundation (and multiple interventions) for how the focus in education can move toward a more holistic, humanistic, and student-centered approach.

Bill Milliken in his book *The Last Dropout* (2007) notes that "Without someone to believe in him, a teenager gets angry and he starts to take it out on other people and himself" (p. 7). Milliken should know: He dropped out of school. His turn-around point? When an adult started to care about him. Milliken writes, "Should I have received unconditional love from my parents? Sure—but like millions of young people, I didn't" (p. 5). The angry and disruptive students you see in your classroom will not become less angry or disruptive until someone—perhaps you—connects with their sense of self and restores it to life. Once armed with shiny, stable containers, students can make decisions that reflect that positive self-image to the world, which in turn will start to build a world that is more apt to support the self.

Let's begin to look at the possibilities of the future by understanding the role the self plays in our ability to make well-informed and thoughtful decisions.

Check In With Your Self

How much thought do you put into your decisions?

__Knee-jerk reactor   __Thoughtful consider-a-tor   __Wing it and pray   __No idea

DECISION MAKING—
THE SINE QUA NON OF SELF SKILLS

When we make a decision, we check in with so many variables: We weigh pros and cons, we consider consequences, various permutations, and alternate possibilities. Ultimately, the one thing we all do subconsciously with nearly every decision we make is that *we check in with who we are.* The ability to make sound decisions, decisions that resonate with the true self, is a skill that develops through a process of self-reflection and trial and error. It becomes a skill that one hones over a lifetime. Your students are in the development stage of their decision-making abilities. Helping them to understand that this is a process that relies on the self will help them to make decisions that feel right and generate a better future for all of us.

When your students become self-aware, fully functioning, contributing members of society, they will make decisions that support their authentic and whole selves. When you teach students to honor that self by reaching and teaching to the self, you help them to make decisions that further their life dreams, goals, and purposes. Furthermore, and this is very important, you are teaching them how to connect, through their choices, with the larger community, and indeed the world. *When students feel worthy and value connections with others, they will want to connect and contribute their worthiness to the world.*

During the Waco, Texas standoff, many lives were lost, including those of young children. But before the fire that ended those lives, dozens of other children were released. Psychologists and trauma therapists who worked with those children discovered something fascinating: They lacked a sense of self. The reason? None of them had been allowed to make one single decision to validate their individuality; all decisions were made for them at every moment—even what utensil to use or when to use the facilities. The children showed physiological signs of trauma when asked to make simple choices (Perry, 2006).

By helping your students tap into their sense of self, you empower them with the ability to tune into their personal decision-making abilities and ultimately empower them to make choices that resonate with who they choose to be. Simply put, helping students understand who they are in relation to all aspects of the self will aid their decision

making. Decisions tell the world who we are as we search for resonance and reassurance that who we are is acceptable. What are your
students projecting in their decisions? How are we helping them project a strong sense of self in keeping with their goals, desires, and
dreams? To understand this process, let us take a brief but closer look
at the many aspects of ourselves that influence our decisions.

Ten Aspects of the Self

(The following information is taken with permission from www
.YourSelfSeries.com.)

Most aspects of the self contribute to our daily decisions. Subconsciously,
we check in with who we are as we choose among friends, social events,
ethics, and even our clothing each day. Below is a list of 10 aspects of the
self that we rely on every moment as we choose how to navigate our path in
life.

Ten aspects of the self on which you rely when you make minor to
monumental decisions are

- ☑ Your emotions
- ☑ Your morals
- ☑ Your past experiences
- ☑ Your psyche
- ☑ Your peer influences
- ☑ Your media influences
- ☑ Your parental influences
- ☑ Your personality
- ☑ Your culture, race, ethnicity, and spirituality
- ☑ Your mind/body connection (your ability to control stress, etc.)

Intervention 9.1: Ten Aspects of the Self

Copy the list above and share it with your students. Then suggest the
following example so they can apply the concept to something relevant.
Explain that each time they ponder a choice (i.e., *Will I go to the movies
with Kristen even though I know it will be past my curfew when I get home? My
parents are always asleep when I get home at curfew so I might not get caught.*),
they subconsciously check in with almost every single one of those self-
aspects listed.

Your emotions *(I will feel guilty for going, but I will have a great time. If the guilt is too overwhelming, I will not go.)*

Your morals *(It would be wrong to lie to my parents.)*

Your past experiences *(My brother did this once and got away with it, so maybe I can, too. But I always feel bad when I let down my parents.)*

Your psyche *(This isn't the way I normally behave. I don't know why I am having such a difficult time with this decision.)*

Your peer influences *(Kristen is begging me to go and I really want to hang out with her.)*

Your media influences *(I am dying to see this movie! It's the hottest movie out there.)*

Your parental influences *(They will be so upset with me if I am not honest.)*

Your personality *(I like to go with the flow, but this feels like I am stuck.)*

Your culture, race, ethnicity, and spirituality *(I was raised to be honest and fair and to respect myself and others.)*

Your mind/body connection (your ability to control stress, etc.) *(I will totally stress over this if I go and then I won't enjoy the movie. Worse, I'll probably eat junk to make me feel better and then I'll feel even worse!)*

These aspects of the self weigh heavily on teens. Sometimes decisions are easy, and they don't consciously go through all of this. But when decisions are more difficult, having a strongly developed sense of self and, indeed, a strong awareness of all these different aspects of the self, helps teens to make decisions that are right for them. Most teens have an innate desire to be productive and contributing members of society and will choose pathways toward that end when they feel worthy and appreciated. This is why reaching that self is so vital: It allows teens to make decisions that will connect them to others and keep them in school.

Decisions and Cognition

Choices include two levels of cognition:

1. The unconscious, intuitive, emotion-based reaction

2. Reflective, thoughtful, and reasoned response

Let us provide an example.
We are about to ask you a few questions. Answer them in order and immediately, please.

- What color is the sky (maybe not now, but always, even when it's cloudy)?
- What do chickens lay?
- What color is snow?
- What do cows drink?

Blue, eggs, white, milk. Milk? Well, it is usually the first response. It falls under category #1 above: unconscious, intuitive response. However, after a quick moment, we jump into #2 above, having realized our oversight. Oops. Water. When we are in solid decision making, we will listen to *both* #1 and #2. We want to know about #1, as it aids in our survival, but we need to consider #2. Both help us choose! Many students have #1 nailed down. In general, we need to help them incorporate #2 more (Willis, 2011a). This is what building an awareness of the self does: It incorporates both intuitive and reasoned responses in making a decision.

Check In With Your Self

Interest, passion, purpose, meaning, commitment, autonomy. Does the work you ask of your students elicit any of these emotions? How might your students feel if it doesn't? If it does?

MOTIVATION

Kids enter school curious, overflowing with imagination, enthusiasm, and creativity. Somewhere at the end of elementary and at the beginning of middle school, those feelings are lost, transformed to boredom and dispassion by the time many reach high school. How is it that we are siphoning all their creativity and passion? Perhaps we have been too focused on extrinsic motivators and not enough on intrinsic motivators. Perhaps then we are failing to support their self well enough so that it feels safe and ready to learn.

As learning becomes more demanding and more distant from the original process, it begins to lack relevance to the student (*Yes, I can read . . . but what does reading Shakespeare do for me?*). As Chapter 5 illustrates, as personal relevance diminishes, so does motivation. Thus, improving motivation means helping kids look at course content in a new way—a more important way to them. This is part of the reason project-based learning is so valuable. Students are able to see the purpose of certain skills in a more meaningful context: *Ah! This is why I want to know about graphs and charts; I can quantify and illustrate my basketball stats to improve my performance.* The more we can relate material to students' dreams and desires, the more likely we will help them to become intrinsically motivated.

In their work on motivation (in which they use the terms *autonomous* versus *controlled* in place of *intrinsic* and *extrinsic*, respectively, because their terms are more self-oriented), Edward Deci and Richard Ryan (2000) cite three needs for motivation to occur:

1. The need to belong and feel connected

2. The need to feel competent

3. The need for autonomy and self-determination

In Daniel Pink's bestselling novel, *Drive* (2009), he suggests many factors leading to motivation, but one in particular: Purpose. Students need to feel that what they are doing/learning has a greater impact. An educator's job is to make sure all four of these needs, and many more, are being met. To do so, simply incorporate the interventions found within these pages, as they all aim to support these intrinsic motivational needs by supporting the self.

Indeed, motivation to do well in any course is increased when students are supported in their passions. Search Institute (2012) has developed the idea of *sparks:* "interests and passions young people have within them that light a fire in their lives and express the essence of who they are and what they offer to the world." The Search research has shown that when children are supported in their sparks, they are less depressed, less worried, less likely to engage in risky behaviors (make better decisions), more satisfied with their lives overall, and do better in school (www.search-institute.org). The message is clear: Support children in their passions, in the areas of their lives that touch their core sense of selves, and those children are not only more resilient but also more motivated to do well overall.

Our message is this: Connect with your students, support their developing identities, help them find personal meaning in what you teach, and motivation will increase. *Catering to the self is not just some idealistic goal for some to incorporate in their curriculum. Rather, it is a vital element in returning passion and the love of learning back to the classroom.* When you make connections with your students, support their sparks, and create a climate that inspires curiosity, you will have motivated them both in school and in life.

> In their paper, "Five Key Ingredients for Improving Student Motivation," Williams and Williams (2011) write, "Include the study of self-information: Just like people everywhere, students are intrinsically interested in the study of information about themselves and about their own personal interests. Instructors need to find creative ways of knowing and incorporating self-information into the classroom" (p. 16).

In summary, below is a list of considerations to improve motivation. (Additional specific interventions can be found in Chapter 5.)

- Clear the pathways to the prefrontal cortex by mitigating stress (Chapter 5). Nobody is motivated to learn when he or she feels stressed.
- Create good student/teacher connections. Remember what Kyla said in Chapter 6? She wanted to do well because the relationship with her teacher mattered to her. Be a dopamine dispenser, reach the self, and make authentic connections to motivate students.
- Rethink grading systems. Think about effort and behavior and kindness, not competition and self-doubt.
- Cultivate a climate free of chaos and fear. Does everyone get along and feel safe expressing thoughts and feelings? If not, try icebreakers and self-discovery work.
- Set long-term goals to improve motivation: When students are asked to contemplate their long-term goals, they begin to see a bigger picture. Teach by example as well. Post your long-term goals for the class: *Four battles of the Civil War by end of the week.* Having the goal front and center reminds students of the purpose.
- Enhance intrinsic motivation through mental imagery and visualization (discussed in Chapter 8).
- Allow students to feel more competent by having them be part of the parent-teacher meetings. This allows them to take greater ownership in their learning.

- Improve self-concepts by having students help out around school. Kids need to feel they are making a difference! A very nice example of this is found here: woosterschool.org/admissions/self-help-program. In Wooster's Self-Help program, students take an active role in the maintenance of their school. As one teacher notes, it does more than just clean the school, it also builds morals and morale.
- Help kids who do not want to be in school by giving them a purpose to be there. For example, Dr. Robert Brooks recounts a successful intervention of several of the most frequently truant students at one school who were asked to take part in a special project. The project? Form a committee to research truancy, ways to improve attendance, and ways to motivate others to attend. They also had to meet every day after school to report their findings to a board of teachers. The students felt empowered, and indeed, showed up to school (they had to run the meeting!) (Brooks, 2013).

Giving Back

The more one forgets himself—by giving himself to a cause to serve or another person to love—the more human he is.

—Victor Frankl

Imagine you take a science course and build a rocket launcher. How will you know if it works? You can go over the wires and check the mechanics, but until you test it, you will not know for sure how it works or even how high it will fly. Likewise, how will students know that their talents and skills are valuable to the world unless they have the opportunity to test them in the world?

This is why finding opportunities for students to give of themselves is essential in completing the development of that solid shiny container. When students have the opportunity to give of themselves and are well received, they are able to *experience* that they are valued. When they experience appreciation and feel valued, their self is bolstered, and they will be more likely to give again in the future. Giving back is thus cyclical in nature: When students give of themselves and receive appreciation from others in return, they begin to appreciate their selves even more, and they continue to give back.

This is how teaching to the self comes full-circle. By affirming that the self is capable of great things, students become more open to giving those great things. They know their rocket launcher works: They will be more likely to continue to refine it and demonstrate its power to others.

Feeling valued for their being and for their talents also contributes to a student's overall sense of purpose, a key indicator of well-being. "Research has shown that having purpose and meaning in life increases overall well-being and life satisfaction, improves mental and physical health, enhances resiliency, enhances self-esteem, and decreases the chances of depression" (Smith, 2013). People who lead purposeful and meaningful lives are far more likely to give back and to receive more joy from that experience than from focusing solely on finding happiness. According to a Gallup Poll, 60% of Americans today feel happy. But according to the Center for Disease Control, "about four out of ten Americans have not discovered a satisfying life purpose" (Smith, 2013).

This book is suggesting you reach and teach to the self to bring forth self-awareness and ignite inner passions and purposes. Finding passions gives life more meaning. More meaning increases well-being and the likelihood that a person will give his or her talents and self to the world. When those talents are well received, well-being increases even more.

> Victor Frankl, author of *Man's Search for Meaning*, found his own life's purpose during the time he spent in a concentration camp. Frankl worked as a therapist while in the camp, helping those who felt life was meaningless. Frankl stresses that we find purpose and meaning when we align our goals with something (or someone) greater than the self (Smith, 2013, p. 2).

To increase meaning and purpose in education, many schools are now incorporating project-based learning and service learning models as they teach core subjects. These self-motivated methods of instruction tap into students' passions for giving back. With the self so focused inwardly during the teen years, helping them focus on other people and organizations not only plants the seed of outreach in their developing minds but allows them to *experience* the value of their beings.

Many ways to help students "give back" exist. Here are a few examples of how to do so:

- Encourage the older athletes to inspire the younger athletes.
- "Commission" the artists to paint the walls in the halls.
- Ask the science whiz to entertain the school with a rocket demonstration.
- Have the mathematically gifted run the school store.

- Seek out the historically inclined to write the school news.
- Encourage the quiet back seat angels to bake breads and deliver them to those in need.

When we encourage students to participate in the many and varied ways they can give to the community, we are both valuing their gifts and encouraging the responsibility each has to give to each other and to society (Milliken, 2007). By nurturing their self development, you also nurture their innate capacity for humanitarian good, thereby tapping into the meaning and purpose each holds for a brighter future.

FINAL INTERVENTIONS

Perhaps what pushes middle school students to concentrate and practice . . . is the unexpected experience of someone taking them seriously, believing in their abilities, and challenging them to improve themselves.

—Tough (2012, p. 121)

This book does not propose a unique idea. Philosophers, educators, and even parents have honored the importance and relevance that teaching to the self affords. Studies conducted 50 years ago taught us the significance of reaching our students on a humanistic level (Davidson & Lang, 1965; Fink, 1965). But, as the study findings and statistics shown here point out, at no time is this philosophy more needed than now. We cannot continue teaching for the next 50 years in the same manner without consequences to our dropout rates, world education standings, and indeed, the emotional state of our children. We have offered many interventions to help you reach your students. However, we leave you with an additional few.

Intervention 9.2: Create a Self Folder for Each Student

In their Self Folders, have students answer the question, Who am I? Let your imagination soar and even ask your students what they would like to add. They may want to include accomplishments outside of school or pictures commemorating proud moments. Perhaps include a roles, goals, and accomplishments chart from each year. Each year, and when they graduate, give them their folders. Not all students are afforded the opportunity to "see" how they have become who they have become. The Self Folder will remain an invaluable asset as students springboard into life: something to remind them how they became who they are and the fact that they have the power to shift and evolve into a new person at any time—the brain is wired for it.

Intervention 9.3: Regularly Celebrate the Self

Don't wait for birthdays as the only time to honor students and their gifts. Celebrate who your students are regularly. Feature quotes of the day from your students in the morning announcements, post pictures on the walls of students helping others—naming the students involved, select students whom you might not have otherwise asked for help to help on a school task, ask to have lunch with them, send appreciation notes home to their parents telling their parents something you appreciate about the students—do anything that says to them, "I see you, and I am grateful that you are here." Make those small appreciations routine and be sure that all students feel equal praise for their efforts.

Intervention 9.4: Incorporate SEL Programs

Many SEL programs exist that help students identify emotions, manage their social selves, and develop responsible choices. Support your school's effort to implement such a program; they will make your job of reaching the self much easier. However, be sure that the program your school chooses digs deep and helps students discover the inner core they so cleverly protect. What curriculums are available that will not only support but also actively seek to develop the self? Organizations such as CASEL, SAHMSA, and Eutopia.org can help you find a program that is right for your organization. Of course, our own program located at www .yourselfseries.com is at the top of our recommendation list as it is a complete self education program for young teens and includes lesson plans with project-based learning (PBL) and service learning (SL) examples. Indeed, many programs exist, but none will be effective until implemented, and moreover, implemented by an educator, such as yourself, who keeps the needs of the self in mind when teaching.

CHAPTER SUMMARY

Check In With Your Self

Which aspect of the self did you identify with the most as you read this book?

Which have you not thought much about until now?

Consider the road we have traveled thus far:

- Early connections pave the way for later social, love, work, and peer relations. When children are unable to connect to their caregivers, their ability to build relationships later in life is hindered. Later relationships with other caring adults can change early habits: *Relationships, not programs, heal people; they bring us together to create common good.*
- The more aware a person becomes (truly able to acknowledge reality even when that reality is unpleasant), the less likely that person is to develop a defensive nature, inhibiting learning (and life) potential.
- When a teacher provides a safe environment so students can attend to an otherwise malnourished self development stage, then healing occurs and the true self emerges.
- When we provide students with skills for emotional management, they are more able to attend to the task of learning and form more constructive relationships with their peers and with adults.
- The brain is building and pruning constantly in the teen years. The experiences we coconstruct with them set the stage for their futures. As Aristotle wrote, "We are what we repeatedly do. Excellence then, is not an act, but a habit."
- Social skills development allows us to bolster a sense of self that is well connected to other beings: a neurophysiological need in all of us.
- The body is intimately connected to the mind. By promoting physical health, we promote not just a strong body, but a stronger *student* body.
- Removing nonacademic barriers to learning through a supportive climate fosters the prosocial skills that positively affect motivation.

We hope that these ideas have resonated within your self, enough so that you may feel empowered to not only try the interventions offered but to offer them to your colleagues and peers as well. We hope you have become inspired. After all, you are teaching and inspiring the next generation who will catapult us to greatness or slip on the slope of fear, shame, and unworthiness. Education needs to shift consciousness to include a mindset of self-awareness, self-discovery, and ultimately positive, supportive, inclusive self-perceptions. We hope you will be a part of that shift.

Recall the container analogy: Each one of your students has a container just waiting to be noticed, polished, and filled with positive self-perceptions. How will you begin their journey toward a greater sense of self and acceptance? What connections will you make? Those that you forge with your students today create their containers, and our world, of tomorrow. Through strong, caring, and authentic relationships with our students, we build a core that is capable of making solid, thoughtful, and positive decisions. We also reignite students' passion for learning and their innate desire to feel worthy. After all, they are all worthy. When we reach them not with just words, but with our hearts, the containers are polished to a more authentic shine and limitless potential.

Who will your students be when they leave your classroom or your school? Who will you be every day that you enter your classroom or your school? We hope this book has inspired you to answer, *a very connected, purposeful, inspired, and passionate self.*

Interventions

Watch the Brene Brown TED talk for your self

Ten aspects of the self

Create a Self Folder for each student

Regularly celebrate the self

Incorporate SEL programs

Quick Reference

Below is a chart with all the interventions throughout this book to remind you of the many ways that you can reach and nurture the self.

Intervention	Notes
2.1 Come Alongside Your Students	
2.2 Reflect Who You Know the Student Is Capable of Being	
2.3 Teach and Promote the Five-Finger Rule	
2.4 Index Cards	
2.5 Support Student Efforts to Connect	
2.6 Share Your Self	
3.1 Object-Oriented Language	
3.2 Validation	
3.3 Mirroring	

3.4	Scaffolding	
3.5	Managing a Group Resistance	
3.6	Intent Versus Content	
4.1	Promote Empathy	
4.2	Know the Language of Bullying in Your School	
4.3	Use Praise Over Punishment	
4.4	Develop a Plan; Define the Endgame	
4.5	Seek to Find Success	
4.6	Index Cards for Temper Management	
4.7	Tap the Desk	
4.8	Be Clear About Expectations	
5.1	Teach Basic Brain Anatomy and Function	
5.2	Journal for Test Success	
5.3	Meditation and/or Focused Breathing	
5.4	Stay on Task	
5.5	Be a Dopamine Dispenser	
5.6	Tap Into the Right Side of the Brain	
5.7	Scaffold	
5.8	Improve Self-Control	
5.9	Assess the Stress	
5.10	Put Information in Context to Increase the Level of Interest	
5.11	Immediate Feedback	
5.12	Lay It on the Line	
5.13	Connect With Students' Style of Learning	

6.1	Telephone	
6.2	Collaborating From Small to Larger Groups	
6.3	Rotations	
6.4	Bridging	
7.1	Community Resources: Variety at a Limited Cost	
7.2	School Teams	
7.3	Activity Breaks	
7.4	Nutrition Assignment	
7.5	Time Management	
7.6	Create Healthful Habits	
7.7	Visualization	
7.8	Mindfulness	
7.9	Meditation	
8.1	Model Empathy	
8.2	Debate Moral Dilemmas	
8.3	Chunk and Reward	
8.4	Pretests and Rewrites	
8.5	PBL to Enhance School Morale	
9.1	Ten Aspects of the Self	
9.2	Create a Self Folder for Each Student	
9.3	Regularly Celebrate the Self	
9.4	Incorporate SEL Programs	

References

Abeles, V. (Producer). (2010). *Race to nowhere: The dark side of America's achievement culture*. Lafayette, CA: Reel Link Films.

Ainsworth, M. D. S., & Bell, S. M. (1970). Attachment, exploration, and separation: Illustrated by the behavior of one-year-olds in a strange situation. *Child Development, 41*, 49–67.

Anxiety and Depression Association of America. (2012). Facts & statistics. Retrieved December 4, 2012, from http://www.adaa.org/about-adaa/press-room/facts-statistics

Baird, A. (2010, August 24). *Best defense against cyber bullies*. Retrieved August 3, 2012, from http://www.scientificamerican.com/article.cfm?id=best-defenses-cyber-bullies

Balfanz, R., & Byrnes, V. (2012). *Chronic absenteeism: Summarizing what we know from nationally available data*. Baltimore, MD: Johns Hopkins University Center for Social Organization of Schools.

Beilock, S. (2011, September). Back to school: Dealing with academic stress. *APA: Psychological Science Agenda, 25*(9).

Bhanoo, S. N. (2011, January 28). *How meditation may change the brain*. Retrieved November 13, 2012, from http://well.blogs.nytimes.com/2011/01/28/how-meditation-may-change-the-brain/

Blair, C. (2012, September/October). Treating a toxin to learning. *Scientific American Mind*, p. 64.

Blodget, A. (2009). *Motivation: Making room for the self in school*. Washington, DC: National Association of Independent Schools.

Bowlby, J. (1988). *A secure base: Parent-child attachment and healthy human development*. London, UK: Routledge.

Brackett, M. A., Reyes, M. R., Rivers, S. E., Elbertson, N. A., & Salovey, P. (2011). Classroom emotional climate, teacher affiliation, and student conduct. *Journal of Classroom Interaction, 46*(1).

Bridgeland, J. M., DiIulio, J. J., Jr., & Morison, K. B. (2006). *The silent epidemic: Perspectives of high school dropouts*. Retrieved from http://docs.gatesfoundation.org/united-states/documents/thesilentepidemic3-06final.pdf

Brody, J. (2012, August 27). *Changing our tune on exercise*. Retrieved August 28, 2012, from http://well.blogs.nytimes.com/2012/08/27/changing-our-tune-on-exercise/

Brooks, D. (2011). *The social animal: The hidden sources of love, character, and achievement*. New York, NY: Random House.

Brooks, R. (2012). The power of mindsets: Nurturing student engagement, motivation, and resilience in students. In S. L. Christenson, A. L. Reschly, &

C. Wylie (Eds.), *Handbook of research on student engagement* (pp. 541–562). New York, NY: Springer.

Brooks, R. (2013, April 10). *The power of mindsets: Nurturing motivation and resilience in students.* Learning & the Brain, one-day symposium, New York, NY.

Brooks, R., & Goldstein, S. (2003). *Nurturing resilience in our children.* New York, NY: McGraw-Hill.

Brown, B. (2011). *The power of vulnerability.* Retrieved August 4, 2012, from http://www.youtube.com/watch?v=iCvmsMzlF7o

Brown, T. (2012). Learner's Edge Consulting. Nashville, TN.

Cacioppo, J. T., & William, P. (2008). *Loneliness: Human nature and the need for social connection.* New York, NY: W.W. Norton & Company.

Chillot, R. (2013, April). Touch louder than words. *Psychology Today*, pp. 54–61.

Clark, L. V. (1960, December). Effect of mental practice on the development of a certain motor skill. *Research Quarterly, 31*(4), 560–569.

Clark, S. (2012). *Sleep better: Eat these five foods.* Retrieved November 13, 2012, from http://www.askmen.com/sports/health_400/468_sleep-better-eat-these-5-foods.html

Combs, A. (1962). *Perceiving, behaving, becoming: A new focus for education.* Washington, DC: Association for Supervision and Curriculum Development, a department of the National Education Association.

Combs, A. (1991). *The schools we need: New assumptions for educational reform.* Maryland University Press of America.

Combs, A. W. (1997). *Interviews with Dr. Arthur W. Combs* [DVD series]. Denver: University of Colorado.

Combs, A. W. (2010). Two views of motivation. In A. C. Richards (Ed.), *Matters of consequence: Selected writings of Arthur W. Combs, Ph.D.* Carrollton, GA: Field Psych Trust.

Davidson, H. H., & Lang, G. (1965). Children's perceptions of their teachers' feelings toward them related to self-perception, school achievement, and behavior. In D. E. Hamachek (Ed.), *The self in growth, teaching, and learning: Selected readings* (pp. 424–439). Englewood Cliffs, NJ: Prentice Hall.

Domestic violence statistics. (2013). Domestic Violence Resource Center. Retrieved from http://www.dvrc-or.org/domestic/violence/resources/C61/

Duckworth, A. (2011, February 2). *The significance of self-control.* Retrieved December 12, 2012, from http://www.pnas.org/content/108/7/2639.full

Dunbar, F. (2008, August). Essential questions: Mining for understanding. *Middle Ground, 12*(1). Retrieved from http://www.amle.org/Publications/Middle Ground/Articles/August2008/tabid/1702/Default.aspx

Durlak, J. A., Weissberg, R. P., Dymnicki, A. B., Taylor, R. D., & Schellinger, K. B. (2011, January/February). The impact of enhancing students' social and emotional learning: A meta-analysis of school-based universal interventions. *Child Development, 82*(1), 405–432.

Dweck, C. S. (2006). *Mindset: The new psychology of success.* New York, NY: Ballantine Books.

Eisner, E. W. (2004). *The arts and the creation of mind.* New Haven, CT: Yale University Press.

Elias, M. J., & Zins, J. E. (2006). Social and emotional learning. In G. G. Bear & K. M. Minke (Eds.), *Children's needs III: Development, prevention and intervention.* Bethesda, MD: National Association of School Psychologists.

Fink, M. B. (1965). Self-concept as it relates to academic underachievement. In D. E. Hamachek (Ed.), *The self in growth, teaching, and learning: Selected readings* (pp. 424–439). Englewood Cliffs, NJ: Prentice Hall.

Firestone, L. (2013). Benefits of mindfulness [Compassion Matters Blog]. *Psychology Today.* Retrieved from http://www.psychologytoday.com/blog/compassion-matters/201303/benefits-mindfulness

Freud, A. (1979). *The ego and the mechanisms of defense.* New York, NY: International Universities Press.

Haber, J. (2007). *Bullyproof your child for life: Protect your child from teasing, taunting, and bullying for good.* New York, NY: Penguin.

Haefner, J. (2012). *Mental rehearsal & visualization: The secret to improving your game without touching a basketball.* Retrieved November 13, 2012, from http://www.breakthroughbasketball.com/mental/visualization.html

Hay, C., & Meldrum, R. (2010, May). Bullying victimization and adolescent self harm: Testing hypotheses from general strain theory. *Journal of Youth and Adolescence, 39*(5), 446–459.

Health scare of the week: The toll of childhood violence. (2012, May 2). *The Week.*

Hofmann, W., & Friese, M. (2011, May/June). Control yourself! *Scientific American Mind.*

Horstman, J. (2009). *The scientific American day in the life of your brain.* San Francisco, CA: John Wiley & Sons.

Immordino-Yang, M. H., & Damasio, A. (2007). We feel, therefore we learn: The relevance of affective and social neuroscience to education. *Mind, Brain, and Education, 1*(1), 3–10.

Infidelity statistics. (2006). *InfidelityFacts.com.* Retrieved from http://www.infidelityfacts.com/infidelity-statistics.html

Jacobs, H. H. (Ed.). (2010). *Curriculum 21: Essential education for a changing world.* Alexandria, VA: ASCD.

Jacobs, H. H. (2011, November 18–20). *Curriculum 21: Essential education for a changing world.* Keynote address at the Learning & the Brain conference, Boston, MA.

Kagan, J. (1984). *The nature of the child.* New York, NY: Basic Books.

Kelland, K. (2011, November 17). *One in 12 teenagers self harm, study finds.* Retrieved November 20, 2012, from http://www.reuters.com/article/2011/11/17/us-self-harm-idUSTRE7AG02520111117

Kiefer, H. M. (2004, January 20). *Empty seats: Fewer families eat together.* Retrieved December 12, 2012, from http://www.gallup.com/poll/10336/empty-seats-fewer-families-eat-together.aspx

Kirman, W. J. (1977). *Modern psychoanalysis in the schools.* Wayne, NJ: Avery Publishing Group.

Lavoie, R. D. (2013, April 10). *The motivation breakthrough: Turning on the tuned out child.* Learning & the Brain, one-day symposium, New York, NY.

LeDoux, J. (2002). *Synaptic self: How our brains become who we are.* New York, NY: Penguin.

Lee, C. L., & Hirschlein, B. M. (1994, Spring/Summer). The relationship between home economics teachers' self-esteem and their classroom interaction. *Journal of Family and Consumer Sciences Education, 12*(1).

Lehrer, J. (2009, May 18). *Don't! The secret of self-control.* Retrieved December 12, 2012, from http://www.newyorker.com/reporting/2009/05/18/090518fa_fact_lehrer?currentPage=1

Lepper, M. R., Greene, D., & Nisbett, R. E. (1973). Undermining children's intrinsic interest with extrinsic reward: A test of the "overjustification" thesis. *Journal of Personality and Social Psychology, 28*(1), 129–137.

Martin, N., & Halperin, S. (2006). *Whatever it takes: How twelve communities are reconnecting out-of-school youth.* Washington, DC: American Youth Policy Forum.

Meditation's health benefits. (2012, November 30). *The Week*, p. 21.

Milian, M. (2010, April 24). *Reading on iPad before bed can affect sleep habits.* Retrieved from http://latimesblogs.latimes.com/technology/2010/04/ipad-kindle-ebook-sleep.html

Milliken, B. (2007). *The last dropout.* New York, NY: Hay House.

The missing piece: A national teacher survey on how social and emotional learning can empower children and transform schools. (n.d.). Retrieved from http://casel .org/2013forum/the-missing-piece/

Moffitt, T., Arseneault, L., Belsky, D., Dickson, N., Hancox, R. J., Harrington, H., . . . Caspi, A. (2010). A gradient of childhood self-control predicts health, wealth, and public safety. *Proceedings of the National Academy of Sciences of the United States of America* [online], *108*, pp. 2693–2698.

National Sleep Foundation. (2012). *Teens and sleep.* Retrieved November 7, 2012, from http://www.sleepfoundation.org/article/sleep-topics/teens-and-sleep

A neglect of mental illness. (2012, March). *Scientific American*, p. 8.

Norden, J. (2007). *Understanding the brain (Course guidebook).* Chantilly, VA: The Great Courses.

Organization for Economic Cooperation and Development [OECD]. (2008). *Education at a glance: OECD indicators.* Retrieved July 1, 2013, from http:// www.oecd.org/education/skills-beyond-school/41284038.pdf

Padesky, C. A. (1990). Schema as prejudice. *International Cognitive Therapy Newsletter, 6,* 6–7.

Perry, B. D., & Szalavitz, M. (2006).*The boy who was raised as a dog: And other stories from a child psychiatrist's notebook—What traumatized children can teach us about loss, love, and healing.* New York, NY: Basic Books.

Pert, C. B. (2006). *Everything you need to know to feel go(o)d.* Carlsbad, CA: Hay House.

Pink, D. H. (2009). *Drive: The surprising truth about what motivates us.* New York, NY: Penguin.

Ravitch, D. (2010). *The death and life of the great American school system: How testing and choice are undermining education.* New York, NY: Basic Books.

Reynolds, G. (2012, April 22). Jogging your brain. *New York Times Sunday Magazine.*

Robinson, K. (2009). *The element: How finding your passion changes everything.* New York, NY: Penguin.

Ryan, R. M., & Deci, E. L. (2000). Self-determination theory and the facilitation of intrinsic motivation, social development, and well-being. *American Psychologist, 55,* 68–78.

Search Institute. (2012). *Research.* Retrieved November 3, 2012, from http:// www.search-institute.org/sparks/research

Segal, J. (1988). Teachers have enormous power in affecting a child's self-esteem. *Brown University Child Behavior and Development Newsletter, 10,* 1–3.

Self. (2011). In *The American Heritage Dictionary.* Retrieved from http://ahdict ionary.com/word/search.html?q=self&submit.x=58&submit.y=16

Seligman, M. E. P. (2011). *Flourish.* New York, NY: Free Press.

Shah, N. (2011, August 10). Half of Texas students in secondary schools have been suspended. *Education Week, 30*(37).

Shapiro, R. J., & Hassett, K. A. (2012, June). *The economic benefits of reducing violent crime: A case study of 8 American cities.* Retrieved from http://www .americanprogress.org/wp-content/uploads/issues/2012/06/pdf/violent_ crime.pdf

Siegel, D. J. (2010). *Mindsight: The new power of personal transformation.* New York, NY: Bantam.

Simon, C. A. (2001). *To run a school: Administrative organization and learning.* Westport, CT: Praeger.

Smith, E. E. (2013, February 6). There's more to life than being happy. *The Atlantic Monthly.* Retrieved from http://www.theatlantic.com/health/ archive/2013/01/theres-more-to-life-than-being-happy/266805/

Sroufe, L. A., Egeland, B., Carlson, E. A., & Collins, W. A. (2005). *The development of the person: The Minnesota study of risk and adaptation from birth to adulthood.* New York, NY: The Guilford Press.

Stiffleman, S. (2010). *Parenting without power struggles.* New York, NY: Morgan James.

Talbot, M. (1991). *The holographic universe.* New York, NY: HarperCollins.

Tough, P. (2012). *How children succeed: Grit, curiosity and the hidden power of character.* New York, NY: Houghton Mifflin.

typoprone. (2009, January 31). *Children full of life (1 of 5)* [Video file]. Retrieved from http://www.youtube.com/watch?v=armP8TfS9Is

University of Minnesota. (2012). *Later start times for high school students.* Retrieved November 15, 2012, from http://www.cehd.umn.edu/research/ highlights/sleep/

Urban Strategies Council. (2007). *The rising costs of incarceration: Criminal investment decisions.* Retrieved December 4, 2012, from http://www.urban strategies.org/programs/csj/documents/CostsofIncarcerationFlyer_08.06 .07_BH.pdf

U.S. Department of Education, National Center for Education Statistics. (2011). *The Condition of Education 2011* (NCES 2011-033), Table A-20-1.

Vega, V. (2012, February 22). *Promising research on meditation in schools.* Retrieved November 13, 2012, from http://www.edutopia.org/stw-student-stress- meditation-schools-research

Villano, K. (2011, April 22). *Moving boys toward learning.* Retrieved September 14, 2012, from http://hillsborough.patch.com/articles/moving-boys-toward- learning

Wagner, T. (2011, November 18–20). *Teaching, learning and leading in the 21st century.* Keynote address at Learning & the Brain conference, Boston, MA.

Weir, K. (2012, January). *The power of self-control.* Retrieved June 28, 2013, from http://www.apa.org/monitor/2012/01/self-control.aspx

Williams, C. C., & Williams, K. C. (2011, August). Five key ingredients for improving student motivation. *Research in Higher Education Journal.* Retrieved December 3, 2012, from http://www.aabri.com/manuscripts/11834.pdf

Willingham, D. T. (2009). *Why don't students like school? A cognitive scientist answers questions about how the mind works and what it means for the classroom.* San Francisco, CA: Wiley.

Willis, J. (2011a, November 18–20). *Brain research to help students develop their highest cognitive level.* Learning & the Brain conference, Boston, MA.

Willis, J. (2011b). Three brain-based teaching strategies to build executive functions in students. Published in *Edutopia* as Staff Blog on October 5, 2011, Part 4 of 7 part series with the same title. Retrieved August 5, 2012, from http://www.edutopia.org/blog/brain-based-teaching-strategies-judy-willis

Winnicott, D. W. (1960). Ego distortion in terms of true and false self. In *The maturational process and the facilitating environment: Studies in the theory of emotional development* (pp. 140–152). New York, NY: International UP Inc.

Yalom, I. D. (1995). *The theory and practice of group therapy* (4th ed.). New York, NY: HarperCollins.

Index

CORWIN

A SAGE Company

The Corwin logo—a raven striding across an open book—represents the union of courage and learning. Corwin is committed to improving education for all learners by publishing books and other professional development resources for those serving the field of PreK–12 education. By providing practical, hands-on materials, Corwin continues to carry out the promise of its motto: **"Helping Educators Do Their Work Better."**